"When I first met one of my favo[...] across from me, took my hand, a[...] That was one of the most profound[...] introductory moments I've ever ex[...] similar encounter when first meeti[...] ....ey. What are you dreaming?" Wow! That one question helped launch what is now known as Phoenix (Community) Roasters, and I am so grateful. To watch Brian Holland, and the team that God has united with him, is to see the manifestation of those two questions. Brian and his team both dream and love well. In reading the account of the founding of this impactful ministry, you too will be inspired to dream and love well, and to believe that 'God takes the responsibility for all the consequences of a heart that's devoted to Him.'"

—Daniel Cline, serving as CEO, Catalyst Conferences

"Our relationship with Phoenix Roasters began almost a decade ago, and it has remained a constant for our ministry ever since. While they craft a great product, their relationships have a lasting impact! Our ministry was able to take a staff of over fifteen baristas to their location for a tour and team building. Wes, the real MVP, taught us all about that tasty little bean that we call coffee and why it can have such an influence on so many lives. Of how it can be used to love someone so well. Isn't that what Phoenix is all about? Loving someone well through a tasty little bean called coffee. We are grateful for them!"

—TC Jones, assistant manager, Atrium Café

"God has equipped Brian with an inspiring and energetic vision for community and global ministry. He loves unconditionally with an unswerving faith and infectious personality. Under Brian's dedicated and passionate leadership, Phoenix exemplifies the New Testament model of church and evangelism forged by the Apostles of Jesus Christ."

—Stewart and Lisa Cink, professional golfer, PGA tour golfer

"Peter stepped out of the boat onto the water because Jesus said, 'Come!' This is a powerful story of answering the call when Jesus says, 'Come!' Brian and his team live out what they talk about in this book as they serve the least in our city, providing hope and dignity through their love and coffee. Their example has not only impacted many of those we get the privilege to serve but also me personally because of their love and care. May this inspire you for the God-sized dreams He has for you."

—James H. Reese, president/CEO, Atlanta Mission

"To me, excellence is a choice. It's choosing to create a better future by going the extra mile. My dear friend Brian Holland and the Phoenix Roasters team choose the extra mile in all that they do, and they're creating a better future for coffee farmers, their workers, and you and I—the coffee consumers. Every cup of Phoenix Roasters coffee represents hope!"

—Stuart Hall, communicator, author, director of Student Leadership, Orange

"We first met Brian at age fourteen when he came into our student ministry at First Baptist Church, Jonesboro, Georgia. His powerful personality made us realize that he would do amazing, adventurous things for God's kingdom—*if* he would listen and respond with a resounding *"Yes!"*

Once Brian said yes to Jesus, he never looked back. Brian's obedience led him to finish his education and begin his work in student ministry. Several years later, God led him to church planting and Phoenix Community of Atlanta was born! From that point, God continues to lead Brian into exciting areas of ministry.

We love being able to be on the sidelines, cheering Brian on as he continues the adventures that come from the incredible joy of obedience to God's direction. It inspires us to do the same … to say "YES" as God whispers His guidance and wisdom into our own hearts and minds.

Two verses come to mind as we pray for Brian:

- Ephesians 2:10: For we are God's handiwork, created in Christ Jesus to do good works, which God prepared in advance for us to do. (NIV)
- Psalm 139:16: All the days ordained for me where written in your book before one of them came to be. (NIV)

—Larry and Anna Lawrence, Lawrence Ministries,
Morristown, Tennessee

"The Phoenix story is a kingdom playground where God's creative children play together and in the process create eternal things. This inspiring book is filled with the personal adventures of people courageous enough to say "yes" to God's call. A treasure trove of practical ministry wisdom."

—Robert (Bob) Lupton, author of *Toxic Charity*, and founder of
FCS Urban Ministries, Atlanta

SAY

How God-Sized Dreams Take Flight

YES

BRITT MOONEY *AND THE*
PHOENIX COMMUNITY OF ATLANTA

IRON STREAM
BOOKS
An Imprint of Iron Stream Media
Birmingham, Alabama

Iron Stream Books
100 Missionary Ridge
Birmingham, AL 35242
An imprint of Iron Stream Media
NewHopePublishers.com
IronStreamMedia.com

Library of Congress Cataloging-in-Publication Data

Names: Mooney, Britt, 1972- author. | Phoenix Community of Atlanta, author.

Title: Say yes : how God-sized dreams take flight / Britt Mooney and the Phoenix Community of Atlanta.
Description: Birmingham, Alabama : Iron Stream Books, an imprint of Iron Stream Books, 2020.
Identifiers: LCCN 2020018488 (print) | LCCN 2020018489 (ebook) | ISBN 9781563094101 | ISBN 9781563094118 (ebook)
Subjects: LCSH: Dreams--Religious aspects--Christianity. | Trust in God--Christianity. |
Missions. | Church work with
minorities--Georgia--Atlanta.
Classification: LCC BR115.D74 M65 2020 (print) | LCC BR115.D74 (ebook) | DDC 277.58/083--dc23
LC record available at https://lccn.loc.gov/2020018488
LC ebook record available at https://lccn.loc.gov/2020018489

ISBN-13: 978-1-56309-410-1
Ebook ISBN: 978-1-56309-411-8

1 2 3 4 5—24 23 22 21 20

This book is dedicated to the broken people of every class, race, gender, status, nationality, and culture with our hope that you rise from the ashes of life to live what God dreams for you.

CONTENTS

FOREWORD

Many years ago I was bow hunting caribou near the Arctic Circle. At the end of the first long day of hunting we had walked many miles and were pretty weary on the way back to camp. As we reached a mountaintop I could see our campsite a couple of miles in the distance.

Thinking of nothing but taking my boots off, I suggested we drop down to the right and cut across a valley instead of taking the longer route we had taken when we set out early that morning.

Our guide said, "Well, we could do that but the alders in that valley are where all the grizzly bears bed down."

My buddy started chuckling and said, "Jeff, don't guide the guide!"

I have thought about that a lot since that day. The guide knows things you don't know. The guide knows where he is going and the obstacles you will encounter along the way. That's why you need him.

Brian Holland and I became friends when we started leading small group Bible studies for homeless men at the Atlanta Mission. We didn't really know what we were doing, and I am not even sure we were qualified to do "it" if we had known. But we had said yes. When God whispers, "Will you do this?" you should always say yes.

We had no idea of the deep and profound relationships we would develop or the amazing changes we would witness in the lives of the men we were walking with.

In fact, in the early days of this ministry, we had to entice the men to attend our classes, so I would buy Chick-fil-A biscuits, and Brian would bring the coffee.

He and a few of his longtime ministry friends had a small business roasting coffee in a warehouse and a big dream about how coffee, of all things, might become the hands and feet of Jesus. Brian had asked me to come meet with his group to hear their dream. They had a dream that they could pay more than fair wages to Jesus-loving coffee growers and to positively affect their lives in their dilapidated areas of housing and education and consequently, by alleviating their poverty, enable them to better take care of their families.

I have heard it said that you can only have influence in the areas you are willing to walk in, and I admired their courage to walk into such a dark and complicated world. But like many small businesses, they had lots of questions about things such as cash flow, margins, workforce, mission, and direction.

After they had finished sharing this dream, they asked for my opinion. (That in itself should show you their level of desperation!) Brian will tell you my reply was my worst joke ever, but in all honesty I wasn't even trying to be funny. I said, "I think you boys just need to keep on grinding it out. It makes your story more interesting and worth listening to. You guys don't know how to get to where you want to go, but God does."

See, once you take the first step and say yes, it's not necessary to know the answers to all the questions that will surely follow, because you are not in charge. But you are definitely not alone. Don't guide the guide. He knows right where He is going.

God Bless,
Jeff Foxworthy

GOD'S STORY

This story is bigger than you think.

It starts with how God rescued the broken and led the rescued to a unique way of doing church, business, and missions, all for the kingdom. All to rescue the marginalized and the misfit.

You will read about church planting, coffee farmers, and mission trips, and those events and principles are important. But it's bigger than that.

At every turn, God gave direction, led the way, sustained during times of waiting, and performed miracles.

God is telling a story. It is an epic story of struggle and redemption and love. It is the only story that matters. The people who join this heroic story are men and women, rich and poor, old and young, Jew and Gentile, strong and weak.

The Acts of the Apostles tells us stories of the early leaders of the church, and those inspired stories build a foundation of truth and testimony. The hero of Acts isn't a human, or group of humans, however. It is the Holy Spirit. Acts records the leading, the movement, and the reality of the Holy Spirit in the lives of people who joined God's story.

The story of Phoenix Roasters is a part of God's story. He initiated, interrupted, and infused every decision and creative idea that led to this place. It belongs to Him.

The way to enter God's story is simple. While in different contexts and situations over thousands of years, the common thread of those who entered God's story is easy to trace.

They all said *yes* to God.

Begins with a Yes

I helped a friend move from their apartment to a new house, one of those "get a bunch of people and a truck and make it happen" kind of days.

My wife and I would soon be leaving for the Republic of Korea to be missionaries. I struck up a conversation with one of the men also helping lift heavy boxes. His jaw dropped when he heard about our plans.

"You and your wife both have good jobs? All your family is here? Everything you love?"

"Yes," I said.

"You'll be making less money, and it could be dangerous?"

"Yes."

His brow furrowed, and he asked an honest question. "Then why are you going?"

I said the only thing that was true. "Because God told us to."

My wife and I didn't know then how God would bless us over the next few years while we served Him in another country. And He did. Immensely. But we heard His voice, said yes, and saw God do amazing things.

It always begins with a yes in Scripture—they built an ark, left a father's house in Ur to wander, hid spies in her own city before a battle, stood before a king without being invited to plead for the innocent, stayed with a young pregnant fiancée when he could have put her away quietly.

Dropped their nets.

Left a great education career in the United States to be a missionary in Korea then returning to be a church-planting pastor working for a coffee company.

The people of Scripture and you and I all start at the same place. We all hear from God and say *yes*.

The Consequences

Maybe it's not that simple. A dream from God may inspire us, but we often shy away from the yes to God.

It looks dangerous and difficult. It will cost us. We could fail.

Hearing from God reveals His love, our worth in His eyes, and more. In the light of His presence, our weakness becomes more real as well. Our insufficiency in the view of His supernatural call.

God asks us to do the impossible because for Him, all things are possible. The supernatural call requires His supernatural grace and power.

The end of God's story is redemptive and will glorify Him. God desires the best for all, and those who say yes to Him also trust that He is responsible for all the consequences of our obedience. The one who calls and empowers is also in charge of the results.

Do we trust Him with the consequences of the yes?

Watch God Work

We can read the stories in the Bible and distance ourselves from those men and women, as though they were different from us. As though they were more worthy or capable. They weren't.

Does God really invade people's lives and radically change them?

Yes.

God begins with the common and the weak, and He calls us into the story. No matter who you are, He's calling you into the story.

Here's a secret, though. We don't say yes to Him only one time. We say yes at several points, every day, allowing Him to change direction and tell the story.

That is the story of Phoenix Roasters.

As you read our story, our prayer is that you will enter into God's story if you haven't already. And if you have, then we pray you are inspired to continue. How you enter and continue is the same.

You start saying yes.

And just watch what God does.

Exploration

The most valuable gift in all existence is revelation from God. Fundamental to saying yes and being in God's story is hearing His voice.

How do you hear his voice? In Acts, the disciples were told to wait for the promised gift of the Holy Spirit (Acts 1:4). Psalm 46:10 tells us to "Be still, and know" that He is God.

It is counter to our consumer culture to turn off the phones, the TV, the noise, and spend time being still and quiet before Him. We get impatient and hate waiting.

We also think it must be in a big meeting or dramatic fashion. Right?

Elijah ran from Jezebel to the mountain, and God told him to stand and wait. God sent the wind, the fire, and the earthquake, but He was in the still small voice that spoke to Elijah (1 Kings 19).

Remove the distractions, and be quiet before Him. Ask Him questions, and you will begin to hear His voice.

Take a moment and write about a time when you knew God spoke to you. What did He say? What was the result?

_____

_____

_____

_____

_____

_____

_____

_____

_____

_____

CHAPTER 1

See the Need

Ginney Holland thought she was the only person awake early that summer morning in 2007.

She shuffled through the hall of Brunswick High School, where 450 kids and youth leaders slept soundly. Several churches had come together for a mission trip in Brunswick, Georgia. Her husband Brian was one of the leaders with eighty of those kids. Like the wives of most ministers, Ginney had traveled down to help chaperone.

Her eyes heavy from lack of sleep with a group of teenage girls, she appreciated the quiet. And she had to go to the bathroom.

A figure rounded the corner from the science lab. She hesitated, surprised to see anyone up and about, but then she relaxed. It was Brian.

With his head lowered and brow furrowed, he didn't see her. His shoulders slumped.

She first assumed the stress and unhappiness at his job contributed to his body language. After several years at a large church in the suburbs of Atlanta, he had developed an obsession for a different kind of church, one that would go to radical lengths to reach those in desperate need. The current church didn't support this obsession, so he felt stuck. Disappointed and discouraged, he wanted to move on to another place, another job.

In looking for other pastoral positions, Brian had been offered the "bigger, better" jobs from churches across the country. The logical next step on the upward ladder of ministry. But Ginney rejected every offer discussed.

Ginney's father had been very ill, and with the need to stay close to family during that difficult time, moving to another church seemed impossible to consider. No matter the package or ministry opportunity offered, Ginney never felt at peace.

Frustrated that he kept entertaining these offers, she once told him what any good minister's wife would say, "No, Brian. Put your big boy britches on, and get to work."

On this Thursday morning in Brunswick, she looked at him a second time. After years of marriage, two kids, and years of successful ministry, she knew her husband well. Better than anyone. Something was different. An aura surrounded him, like the edges of an unfocused lens. His face and countenance told a different story.

Her eyes narrowed, focused on his. He blinked and looked up at her.

Ginney sniffed. "What is wrong with you?"

It took him a moment to answer. "We're leaving."

Peace washed over her, a supernatural calm from God, and she knew in the depth of her soul that no matter what Brian would say next, her answer would be yes.

She asked the most logical question. "Where are we going?"

"We're going to start a church."

"Where?"

Brian said, "Pepperoni's Pizza."

She put her hands on her hips. This was the first time she'd heard this. Phil, the owner of Pepperoni's, a pizza place, employed and worked with at-risk kids in the community. But he was also known as an atheist. At least that was the rumor. Brian had no financial support to start a church. No congregation. No backing from any organization. This carried a mountain of risk. Maybe impossible.

While she stared at him, she saw the dream in his heart. And what she saw touched her own. It was now her dream too.

Ginney stood up straight and nodded. "Okay."

Neither should have been surprised; Brian had decided to follow God without conditions almost twenty years earlier.

The Pretender

The party in the house raged at five in the morning on May 2, 1988. Brian shared the house with his brother while attending Mercer University, at the campus in Atlanta. Brian's girlfriend stayed over so much, she might as well have lived there too. The air filled with smoke while college students took part in drugs and alcohol and each other.

Brian walked through the party, drunk and high. His people. His place. He smiled at friends and acquaintances.

Music blared from the stereo. Jackson Browne's "The Pretender." A great album. The lyrics caught his attention.

Moving through the house downstairs, the words rang in his ears. *Who's the pretender? Who is he talking about?*

A voice shouted in his heart and mind. *You're the pretender.*

He froze. His eyes bulged. Something inside of him shook. *Me. I'm the pretender.*

Once he could tear his feet from the carpet, he ran. He stumbled up the stairs to his room and closed the door. *That was God. He spoke to me.*

Brian turned and scanned the room, the chaos, the disorder. *What can I do? I need a Bible. Do I have a Bible?* His mother taught Sunday school, and his father led the missions team at the church Brian grew up in, but he didn't know if he had a Bible. He had removed all that from his life. Now he needed one.

He remembered his grandfather had given him one recently. He always gave Brian a pocket-sized New Testament every time they parted. Brian had taken it, to be kind, but he had forgotten it like all the others. Where was it now?

Drawers ripped open. He fell to his knees to look under the bed. Turning over a laundry basket, there it was. It must have tumbled out of his pants pocket and settled in the bottom.

A cheap, green Gideon's New Testament with Psalms and Proverbs. The Bible he had thrown away he now gripped with white knuckles.

He did a dangerous, desperate thing. Opening the little book, he fumbled with it and almost ripped the thin pages. He put his finger on a random spot.

Proverbs 2:6–15. He read in his drunken, drugged stupor …

For the LORD grants wisdom! From his mouth come knowledge and understanding. He grants a treasure of common sense to the honest. He is a shield to those who walk with integrity. He guards the paths of the just and protects those who are faithful to him. Then you will understand what is right, just, and fair, and you will find the right way to go. For wisdom will enter your heart, and knowledge will fill you with joy. Wise choices will watch over you. Understanding will keep you safe. Wisdom will save you from evil people, from those whose words are twisted. These men turn from the right way to walk down dark paths. They take pleasure in doing wrong, and they enjoy the twisted ways of evil. Their actions are crooked, and their ways are wrong.

Proverbs 2 read like a checklist of his life, all the ways he lived, all the choices he made. None of them good.

I may have a serious problem. He was not wise, not according to this. Feeling small and lost, he stood and looked up at the ceiling.

But, God, I thought You and me had an understanding.

God replied, *I don't know you.*

Brian's heart shattered at the words, the accusation, the sorrow. The longing of love within that statement.

With a deep breath, he spoke into the air.

"God, if You want me, You can have me. I'm done with me. If You take my life, I'll follow You the rest of my life."

God did want him, as He wants everyone.

The Confession

Soon after, convicted about all he had done, Brian went to talk to his parents, Tommy and Mimi Holland.

These people were his heroes, pillars in the church and the community, successful and revered by many.

And he had stolen from them. Lied to them. For his drug addiction.

He stood in their house and told them everything he had done. He didn't know if they could forgive him, but he asked anyway.

While his mother wept, her chest heaving with sobs, his father, not a big man physically but a giant of integrity and love, stood over Mimi protectively and said, "Well, son. You've told us a lot. You may have lost your inheritance. Now you can get out of my house."

Brian nodded and left, not knowing what would happen. But in that moment, he realized something. He didn't beg, cast blame, or manipulate. He took all responsibility for his actions. He was no longer that old person, the addict, the one to twist the situation for his own benefit. That was different. He was saved.

After thinking and praying, Tommy and Mimi Holland didn't disown him, however. They gave him an opportunity to win back their trust with strict boundaries and rules to follow. Brian did. And over time, the relationship repaired and restored.

In the next few years, Brian became a youth minister and reached out to people with the message of a loving Heavenly Father for everyone. Everyone.

A Different Kind of Church

The desperate, needy people waited in the hallway of the church office in the spring of 2006. Not in the main lobby, where they could be seen, but around the corner. They came on Tuesdays, often the same people, between 11:00 a.m. and 12:00 p.m. to get help from the church. People from the community. Neighbors.

The benevolence hour.

Brian hurried past them from his office to the main sanctuary. The needy people averted their eyes. He gave them a courtesy nod as he passed them by.

As he had learned in two decades of ministry, most churches had a benevolence hour, whatever they might call it. It wasn't advertised, so the weekly ministry didn't have a name. Brian's own church didn't call it anything. But in every fellowship, there was a time set aside for the needy to come and ask for assistance.

He didn't pause because he didn't want to get roped into helping someone. As the youth pastor of a massive suburban church near Atlanta, the other ministers would send him the hard cases. The ones deep in crisis.

That was easy to understand. Brian told his testimony boldly, a testimony of his own brokenness and shame, how he had turned to drugs, alcohol, and sex as a young man, dying slowly from within. And the Lord Jesus Christ had spoken to him, loved him, and saved him. If anyone could understand the hard cases, it was Brian.

While he hurried past, he did wonder about those people. He never saw them at worship on Sundays. *How come these people come every Tuesday for the benevolence hour but not on Sunday for worship?*

And just like in May 1988, God took a nonchalant thought as an opportunity to speak.

Because you can't afford them.

This seemed ludicrous. The church was large, full of middle- and upper-middle-class families. He knew the budget.

Not money, God corrected. *You can't afford the leadership and time it takes to see the desperate and broken transformed.*

His mind began to reel. Jesus had transformed lives and raised up leaders during His three active ministry years on earth. The Father sent Him as a model. How did Jesus do it?

He spent a lot of time with them. Every day. For three years.

Brian sat down with a calculator and did some math. Three years, with 365 days in each year. That's 1,095 days. Assuming twelve hours a day, that would be …

Jesus spent 13,140 hours with twelve men. Not thousands of people. Twelve. One who still betrayed Him. Another denied Him. Several hid. Before they were given the Holy Spirit, sure, but there it was. The cost of time.

The number reminded Brian of a book he had read recently by Malcom Gladwell called *Outliers*. In that book, Gladwell theorized that it took 10,000 hours of time to master something. Anything.

Continuing with his math kick, Brian wondered what a Christian "rock star" would look like in his church. Ten-minute devotional each day? Most didn't do that. And of course, an hour a week in the service on Sunday. That was two hours a week of time "with God." Taking those numbers, how long would it take the modern "rock star" Christian to get the same time with Jesus the disciples had? The ones who turned the world upside down?

By Brian's math, it would take 126 years.

Whatever someone might think of the numbers, the principle held. The only way for broken people to experience change was life on life. This was Jesus' model. For a pastor, that meant larger amounts of time with a smaller group of people. People with serious issues. People in crisis. The addicted, the underresourced, the broken.

The people Jesus hung out with. The ones He sought out. The ones the religious ignored.

No wonder they don't come on Sunday.

For those in the benevolence hour, they were only known by their need. After having to admit their failures or lack of resources, how they weren't good enough, the church administrator would appear from his office and announce who got what.

Humiliating. Lacking human dignity. This was their introduction to the church.

And beyond that, the gap between the needy and the rest of the church was striking. The church building spoke of wealth and opulence, fine carpet and padded pews. The business casual of the upper middle class waited around every corner. Even if someone from the benevolence hour mustered the courage to come on a Sunday, would they feel like they fit in? Probably not.

The current system wasn't working, not for these people. It couldn't afford the time and emotional energy that led to life transformation. What system or model would?

A different kind of church.

The church would have to be intentionally small to encourage deep relationships, where the congregation could see the vulnerability and example of the pastor. It had to be a place where broken and burned-up people would be valued, wanted. Where the broken would learn to take care of one another. Dignified. No respecter of race or nationality. A benevolence-hour church.

Brian listed the types of people who needed to be reached in the community, ones that wouldn't walk into the doors of his current ministry.

The broken, hurting, desperate, addicted, marginalized, under-resourced people.

Where was the church for those people? One that followed the vision God began to birth in His heart?

Brian didn't know, but he wanted to be part of that church.

Exploration

The moment of salvation, the beginning of our intimate relationship with the Father, is a radical yes moment, committing our lives to follow him.

With Phoenix ministries, we adopted a method from missionary Ying Kai of sharing our story in three words. Just come up with and remember three words; this framework allows us to expand our stories as much as needed when we share.

1. *First Word*: What was your life like before you said yes to God and committed to following Him?
2. *Second Word*: What happened to you in the time you knew you said yes to God?
3. *Third Word*: What is your life like now that you are following God?

For example, my three words are—*unfocused* (didn't know who I was or wanted to be in life), *commitment* (God called me to stop "playing church" and fully commit to him), and *purpose* (I have a purpose in every situation or endeavor: to love as Christ loved).

Brian Holland's three words are—*bondage* ("I lived in bondage to secrets no one knew about me"), *freedom* ("I was freed from shame and guilt when I received the love and forgiveness of Jesus"), and *purpose* ("After I realized I could share my experience and help free others from their own, it galvanized my purpose in life").

Take some time to formulate your three words. Write down your three words and a sentence about why you chose each word.

CHAPTER 2
What Are You Dreaming?

A couple years before getting the vision for the Phoenix Community of Atlanta, Brian had been teaching a men's Bible study at the larger church. Two of the verses central to the study began to convict him.

> Come to me, all of you who are weary and carry heavy burdens, and I will give you rest. Take my yoke upon you. Let me teach you, because I am humble and gentle at heart, and you will find rest for your souls. —Matthew 11:28–29

> But if we are living in the light, as God is in the light, then we have fellowship with each other, and the blood of Jesus, his Son, cleanses us from all sin. —1 John 1:7

Both verses speak of intimate fellowship with God, and Brian didn't feel as though he lived in the presence of God. He would get close, but then he would back away, allowing the enemy to beat him down with guilt and shame. Brian never felt he could get even. He kept working to prove himself to God and others.

Here he was teaching the ideas of forgiveness and intimate fellowship. Shouldn't he learn to experience them?

He knew where he had to start. The source of his guilt and shame. A secret he had never shared with anyone. The secret that led to his drug and alcohol abuse.

One week when Brian, his brother, and his father went on a golfing trip, the secret erupted from Brian to his father.

"Dad, when I was five years old, our neighbor invited me up to his room to play cards." The neighbor was popular and a great athlete in the high school. "But we didn't play cards. He molested me."

Tommy Holland began to sob. He violently shook with anger and had to pull the car over. Brian's father cursed and expressed his desire to beat that man up.

Seeing his father that angry made Brian feel protected. The secret was exposed, and he received love and compassion from his father. The moment changed his life. He felt free from that guilt and shame.

Secrets have power in darkness, Brian teaches now. He knows because he's lived it and experienced the effects. Born of trauma, lies spoken by the enemy are mistaken as truth. As part of the lie, we hide those secrets, lock them down in the vault of our hearts, and live out of guilt and shame, projecting life to others but dying on the inside.

The experiences of brokenness and the healing love of the Heavenly Father—and his earthly one—were formative for Brian. His own brokenness gave him a heart for others. Where some in the Christian walk might only see the outward effects like addictions, Brian knew the kind of pain that lingered beneath the surface.

In a desire to take away the power of secrets, Brian often shares his story of being abused and molested as a child. It is a part of his three-word story, which also declares the victory of God's love over the abuse. Almost every time he tells it, people approach him and say, "I've never told anyone this, but that happened to me too."

With that heart for the broken, Brian continued to work toward starting a different kind of ministry for those who needed to rise from the ashes.

Start Your Church

Greg Sweatt rolled his eyes and said, "You might as well go on and start your church," as he and Brian sat over hot plates of Mexican food the summer of 2006.

Brian shook his head. "No, man. I'm telling you, the church is in. They're going to go for it."

He had gone to the head pastor at his church, a good friend and ministry partner for ten years, and presented an idea. After getting the vision of the benevolence hour church, and prayer and brainstorming, God had given Brian the name—Phoenix Community. He had added the name of his current church to the moniker.

He made the presentation with PowerPoint and printed out the pages so everyone could sit and see the info and vision: *Let's use the mission house on church property with its huge living room to start meeting on Sunday morning with the broken and destitute in our community, the ones who don't feel like they'd fit into the larger church.*

I'll be the pastor of that part, and the head pastor and I will work on messages together. And as the broken get better, rise from the ashes like the phoenix, then they can transition into the main service.

Here at the Mexican restaurant, his good friend Greg, a youth pastor from another large church in the area, said, "They won't do it."

"No, they will," Brian said. "We're in the middle of defining our core demographic. We have to make some major changes anyway. The head pastor gave me permission to get a core group together of ten people to pray and dream this vision together. These are people who have gone to bat with me over the years for the broken and hurting people that came to our church. It's happening—a church for people like Alex and Susan."

Alex and Susan, a young couple addicted to crack cocaine, had come into contact with Brian earlier that year. Brian and Ginney took them in and let them live in their house. Emily, Brian's daughter, moved into her brother's room so the couple could have space.

Once Brian found out they weren't actually married, however, Alex slept on the couch until they could put together an official wedding ceremony with rings, a dress, everything. Brian even secured Alex a job at the church. Things were looking up.

Then payday came, the worst day for addicts. Alex called in sick, and after days of being sick, Brian and the church realized he had been using again. Alex ended up losing his job because the church couldn't have a crackhead working there. Alex and Susan spiraled until two men from the Phoenix Community discovery team had to drop them off at a homeless shelter on the south side of Atlanta.

"You haven't heard from them again," Greg said, rummaging through the chip crumbs in the bowl at the center of the table.

Brian sighed. "Yeah, but those are the kind of people we could keep around in the right church. We could really help them."

Greg flagged down the waitress and asked for more chips. Turning his attention back, he said, "Brian, you're gonna have to start your own church. It ain't never gonna happen where you're at."

"No, Greg. It's going to be fine."

Don't You Know?

Brian stood off to the side in a reception room at First Baptist Atlanta (FBA) like a wallflower at a middle school dance that fall in 2006.

The youth pastor at FBA, who is a good friend of Brian, had invited several youth pastors from local churches to a luncheon where Dr. Charles Stanley, the head pastor of FBA, was to speak and mingle with everyone.

The youth pastor, a giant of a man, stood next to Dr. Stanley, peered over the crowd, and caught Brian's eye. "Brian!" He waved him over. "Come on! You want to meet Dr. Stanley?"

The truth was Brian didn't really want to. Stanley had been struggling in private and public ways through his divorce. Being such a major figure in the church world and Atlanta, Stanley had been the subject of discussion and judgment for the previous few months.

But Brian couldn't say no to his friend, not with him waving and Dr. Stanley glancing over. Brian walked through the other youth pastors and stood in front of Dr. Stanley.

Stanley appeared old and stressed, thin with almost translucent skin. He looks like Lo Pan from *Big Trouble in Little China*, Brian recalled.

When he was introduced, Stanley reached out. "Hi, Brian." They shook, and Stanley's long fingers wrapped around Brian's hand. Stanley looked Brian straight in the eye. "What are you dreaming?"

Brian blinked and stammered. "I think God's calling me to start a church." It just came out.

Stanley squinted at him. "What's keeping you from doing that?"

It was like Stanley's hand carried some sort of truth serum. The answer poured out before he could stop it. "I'm afraid."

"What are you afraid of?"

Brian thought of his church, his friends, his community, the security of the job at a big church. His kids were still young. Could he uproot his family from their community? "Of everything I have to lose."

Dr. Stanley's grip grew firmer, and he leaned in close, looking straight into Brian's soul. "Well, Brian, don't you know that God will take responsibility for all the consequences of a heart that's fully devoted to him?"

Time seemed to stop, the room quiet all of a sudden. Too quiet. "Dr. Stanley, if I ever knew that, I forgot."

In a daze, Brian didn't know how the conversation ended, but those words haunted him.

Don't you know that God will take responsibility for all the consequences of a heart that's fully devoted to Him?

Did he?

The Big No

In May 2007, the head pastor sat Brian down in his office. "I'm sorry, Brian. But we won't be doing Phoenix Community, your benevolence hour church. We want you to still be our youth pastor, though. Do you think you can do that?" The pastor smiled at him, in what Brian could only assume was an attempt to be encouraging.

The church had been going through a process of streamlining the programs of the church, cutting away all the extra and unnecessary ministries to do the important things well.

Of course, that meant everyone fought like kingdom come for their own program to stay, defending its importance, how central to the church their ministry was.

In the midst of the process, Brian kept telling the head pastor and the staff, *but the hurting and the broken, the Phoenix people, those were the people Jesus went after. That's where Jesus went to build His church. Shouldn't we?*

After a year of prayer and discussion and dreaming and casting vision, here Brian sat in the office and was told—flatly, simply—no.

He didn't know how to react. He didn't know what to say. Could he still be the youth pastor?

Even though his heart burned with a different vision, he said, "I can. I guess."

Are You Christians?

Even discouraged and deflated, the youth pastor still had work to do.

Brian and Ginney took their eighty students down to Brunswick, Georgia, on a mission trip the summer of 2007. After getting everyone settled in on Monday, July 16, Brian took his wife out to lunch on Norwich Street. They had seen an interesting sign that said Duke's BBQ & Car Wash. July 16 was their son's birthday, which they were missing, and his name was Duke. Brian and Ginney thought they could eat there and maybe get a T-shirt for their son.

Duke's BBQ & Car Wash was in an old bank building retrofitted for a restaurant. They enjoyed their time together and the barbeque, and they got in their car to leave.

A large man appeared at Brian's window and leaned into the car. "You folks are Christians, aren't you?"

Awkwardly, Brian and Ginney nodded.

The man introduced himself as Duke, the owner of the establishment. "I could tell you were Christians. Will you pray for me?"

Brian said, "Sure. What can we pray for you about?"

"I told God that if he would give me this business, I would use it to take care of my family. But I find myself worshipping this business more than the God who gave it to me."

The teaching series for the week during the youth mission trip was on obedience. A timely word for Brian and Ginney.

They prayed for Duke, and Brian felt God prompt him to ask Duke a question. "Do you cater? Have a portable grill or something?"

"Yeah, I cater."

"I'm taking a group down to St. Simons on Wednesday, our day off. Would love to pay you to come out and grill for us."

"No problem," Duke said. "But I need you to come with me to buy the meat on Wednesday."

Brian said, "Of course. Looking forward to it."

Work Harder

Where do you take kids on the day off during a mission trip? The mall, of course.

Walking around the mall that Wednesday, Brian's phone dinged. He pulled it out of his pocket. It was an email from the head pastor to the staff concerning the painful "simple church" process they had been involved in for nearly six months.

"Because of everyone's inability to simplify our church, I am telling you what you're going to do," the email stated. "We are going to do everything we've ever done, but we're going to *work harder* at it."

Brian's face fell, and his heart sank deep within his chest.

I can't work any harder.

Dejected, he had to meet his new friend Duke to pick up the meat.

Brian pulled up to Duke's BBQ & Car Wash to meet a young man he found out was Duke's son.

"Are you Duke's only son?" Brian asked.

The young man smirked. "No, sir."

"How many children does Duke have?"

"Sir, you'd better ask Duke that."

Brian got into the truck with Duke and sat on the passenger side. "Your son said to ask you how many children you have."

"Oh, Brian, you better put your seatbelt on for that question."

Brian put his seat belt on.

Duke's Story

"I've got twenty-four children—eighteen boys and six girls—by multiple different women."

"Wow. What's the story behind that?"

They pulled up to Harvey's Grocery Store and Butcher. Duke put the truck into park.

"I dropped out of school in second grade and started selling drugs."

"Second grade?"

"I was a brand-new teenager when I started having children. I was notorious in Brunswick as a dealer, running drugs up and down the East coast. The older I got, the more trouble I caused and the further I traveled. I got arrested in North Carolina and got a lot of time at the North Carolina federal pen.

"After I'd been in jail a while, I started praying, 'God, kill me. Kill me!'

"God said, *but I don't even know you.*"

I don't know you.

The same thing God had said to Brian nearly twenty years before in 1988. The night he gave his life to God.

Brian took off his baseball cap, leaned over, and began to weep. He blubbered and sobbed, snot coming out everywhere. It was as though his heart had been shoved into a light socket.

Duke continued his story.

"I asked God, 'How do I know You?'

"God said, *pick up your Bible.*

"I told God, 'I can't read.'

"*Pick up your Bible.*

"So I picked up my Bible.

"*Open your Bible.*

"'But I can't read.'

"*Open your Bible.*

"I opened my Bible.

"*Read your Bible.*

"'I can't read!'

"*Read your Bible.*

"I looked down, and I could read every word on the page."

Brian's chest heaved as he groaned in emotion, drunk in the Spirit, like getting saved all over again.

"I gave my heart to Jesus, Mr. Brian.

"Not long after that, they brought a murderer in to be my cell-mate. He had tattoos like teardrops on his face of all the people he killed. He started getting more aggressive and violent.

"I was at my post working, and I said, 'Lord, this man's gonna kill me tonight. You gotta move me back to my family.'

"The Lord asked, *do you trust Me?*

"I told Him I did.

"*You do everything I tell you, and I'll move you home.*

"I go back to my cell, and this man was sitting on the edge of the bunk with a letter in his hand. I ask him, 'What are you reading?'

"The murderer looked up and said, 'I don't know. I can't read. Can you read?'

"I said, 'Yes, I can read.' The man handed me the letter. I read it. 'It's a letter from your sister. It says you need to get saved.'

"The murderer said, 'Do you know how a person is to be saved?'

"I said, 'Yes. Get on your knees.'"

Brian balked at the bravery of telling a murderer to get on his knees. How many people had the man told to get in that position before pulling the trigger?

"I put my hand on his back," Duke continued the story to Brian, "and my hand on the ceiling. When my hand touched the top of the cell, it was like electricity went down my arm and into his back. Something like a watermelon started raising off of his back. It was all the evil spirits in this man, and they started coming out of him. Then he began confessing all his murders.

"And when we got done, he prayed to be saved.

"I lay down on my bunk, exhausted.

"Early in the morning, I heard the jailer knock on my cell. I had forgotten God's promise.

"The jailer said, 'Duke Harris! You're being transferred tonight to Jessup, Georgia.' That's one county over from my family in Brunswick.

"After I got transferred, I started praying that if God would give me a business, I would take care of my children. All of them. And when I got out, I had a bucket and a sponge, and I started washing cars. And now I have barbecue too."

Brian took deep breaths and wiped the snot and tears from his face, taking more than a minute or two to get composed enough to talk. "You have to tell this to my kids tonight."

"Let me tell you something about your kids! Lord says he'll give them whatever they ask for, but their problem is, they have remained silent. This is a silent generation. God is ready to pour out his blessing, but they've remained silent."

Brian knew that the kids in his youth group were not the only ones who were guilty of remaining silent.

Tell Phil I Sent You

Duke spoke to the kids that night, and when Brian went to bed, the words had shaken him. *God is ready to pour out his blessing, but they've remained silent.*

I've remained silent, Brian thinks.

God speaks. *Don't be silent. Will you ask Me?*

Okay. What do You want me to do?

I want you to start the Phoenix Community of Atlanta.

That was the first time God had given him the whole name like that.

Brian tried to stall. *Where? You have to give me a place.*

Go to Phil at Pepperoni's. Tell him I sent you.

Um. Phil's an atheist.

You tell him I sent you.

Should I quit before I talk to him? Or wait just in case he says no and I don't lose my job?

Brian knew the answer before he asked.

Quit.

He spent a night with God's burden on his heart, and the next morning, the first person he saw in a dim and empty hall was his wife Ginney.

"What's wrong?" she asked him.

"We're leaving."

"Where?"

He told her what God told him.

She hesitated, nodded, and said one word. "Okay."

Exploration

"Hello, Brian," Stanley said. "What are you dreaming?"

What are you dreaming? What is the vision God has given you? Salvation is not the only time we say yes, not the only time we step out. He gives us purpose and direction, spiritual gifts. The young will see visions; the old shall dream dreams (Acts 2:17). He has visions and dreams for each of us.

God's call is universal to make disciples, but it is also unique. Like a thumbprint, we are each made unique. For each person, the way we fulfill the universal call is different because of how God has made us.

What is the dream that burns in your heart and won't go away? Is it connected to your three-word story? Often it is.

Take a moment and journal your answers to these questions.

_____

_____

_____

_____

_____

_____

_____

_____

CHAPTER 3

Taking a Leap

"Leaving? You can't leave!"

Brian and Ginney started telling people. They began with their close friends, a handful in the church, and those friends begged them to stay. Brian and Ginney spoke of God's call on their life for this new church. In order to ensure no division or conflict with the current fellowship, Brian and Ginney made it clear they weren't inviting anyone to come with them.

But they hadn't told the head pastor yet.

Brian heard from God about the Phoenix Community of Atlanta on July 18, 2007. Sunday, July 31, Brian asked if he and Ginney could sit and talk with the head pastor and his wife.

"Sure," the pastor said. "We can have dinner together or something."

"Maybe we should just meet first," Brian said.

The four of them met in the offices at the church. The pastor smiled at him. "So. What's going on?"

Brian looked at this man who had been his friend for the past eleven years. They were like family, like brothers. They had served in the trenches together.

But he had to say it.

"We're leaving."

The pastor's face went blank. "What?"

"I'm leaving to start a church."

The room grew tense and quiet. Time stretched. "What church?"

"The Phoenix Community of Atlanta."

Brian knew that much. But then the pastor began asking questions he didn't have answers to. "Where you going to go?"

Brian hadn't talked to Phil yet. "I don't know."

"Who's coming to your church?"

The pastor and his wife were visibly upset. Shocked. Blindsided.

How could that be? This was all I was passionate about for the last year.

Brian shrugged. "The Phoenix people? The broken and destitute. No one may show up."

"You have any support? Any money?"

"No."

The pastor leaned in with pleading eyes. "How … how can you just leave?"

He knew the answer to that. "God's called me to do this. I have to."

The pastor shifted in his seat, took a deep breath. "You thought about when?"

He had. "I thought maybe I could finish through August. The back-to-school retreat is the biggest event of the year, and I could go out with a bang and leave after that retreat." He paused. "I know I'm supposed to preach Sunday, August 12"—the one time the youth pastor got to address the whole church in the main service—"but I don't have to do that."

The head pastor worked through another long hesitation, his face pensive. "Okay. I think that'll be fine."

They closed their conversation as four good friends, brothers and sisters. They cried and prayed together.

Monday morning staff meeting was different.

Brian walked into the room with all the pastors and administrative staff, and the head pastor got everyone's attention. Brian was about to sit down.

"Well, Brian has a big announcement."

Brian's breath caught, and his rear hovered over his seat for a moment before he settled. "Uh. I do?"

"Yep," the pastor said. "Go ahead and tell everyone what you're doing."

Brian looked around the room at several close friends he had wanted to tell privately. Especially his secretary. He swallowed hard. "Um. I-I'm leaving to start a church."

Gasps and squeals of surprise erupted in the room. The secretary looked at him with wide eyes of betrayal.

The head pastor calmed the room. "Brian was supposed to preach on the twelfth, but he's not doing that. That will be his last day."

Brian's jaw dropped. Two weeks. His last day was in two weeks. And he wouldn't get to do one last back-to-school retreat. But what could he say? "Okay."

Phil's Story

Brian contacted Phil at Pepperoni's the next day to set up a meeting. They met that week in the afternoon lull between lunch and dinner at the pizza restaurant.

The tables at Pepperoni's each had a clear top with a decorative theme underneath the glass. Different sports or hobbies were represented. Brian and Phil sat at the Stewart Cink Masters Golf Tournament table.

Brian poured out his story, talking for an hour about what God had told him to do and what kind of church he was going to start for broken and hurting people.

The community knew Phil as the kind of man who took in the broken kids, the kids who were trying to get off drugs or had gotten out of jail. The down-and-outs. He hired them in his pizza place, taught them business, mentored them. He was patient and tough.

Brian concluded his rambling pitch. "And I think God's calling me to start the Phoenix church here on Sundays when you're closed."

Phil, the supposed atheist, leaned back and rubbed his chin. "You've told me a lot, Brian. Can I tell you my story?"

"Of course. Please."

"I grew up in a Catholic church in a northern town in Michigan. I watched my mother go to church every Sunday and give money we didn't have to a church that didn't need it. Then I watched the church ignore the people in the community who were desperate for it."

Phil leaned forward. "Brian, it's not that I don't believe in God. I just don't believe that's the way God wants it. But the kind of church you're talking about, I'm interested in that."

The Phoenix Community of Atlanta had a place to meet.

Two weeks later, there was a reception at the old church, the big church, a thank you. They gave Brian a plaque that said, "For eleven years of faithful service to Brain Holland." *Brain.* They'd misspelled his name.

The ladies that gave him the plaque wore a horrified look. "Oh! We're so sorry! Give it back to us. We'll get it fixed!"

Brian grinned at them. "Naw. It's good. Perfect just the way it is."

First Sunday

The first Sunday for the Phoenix Community was September 7, 2007. While the time seemed short, Brian and his family burst with excitement. Unable to stop talking about it, Brian and Ginney invited everyone. For two years or more, they had rarely invited anyone to church. After all that time, they were finally able to be a part of the church they had been dreaming about. The dream had become a reality.

Would anyone come? It didn't matter. The Phoenix Community was born with a broken-down screen and an old projector. But the soda from the machine was free. That was a big bonus.

People did show up. Friends, family, those excited about the new vision, a church that was real and had a heart for those broken people Jesus gravitated toward. The "leadership" met and laughed and prayed together. Who was the leadership? Everyone. Anyone.

Brian grew up in church and was now a pastor. Those decades of experience taught him that the majority of those who attended church were given hundreds of truths every year—from Sunday sermons to Sunday school lessons to Bible studies and more. How many did they remember? Most retained none, a few one or two.

Over twenty years of Brian's ministry had also shown him that most of the people who attended church knew about Jesus, but they didn't have the evidence of life change from relationship with Jesus, the Father, and the Holy Spirit.

What if the Phoenix Community focused on teaching a handful of truths every year, delving deeply into those ideas over weeks? What if knowing God and developing the experience of a relationship with Him became the focus of the community instead of information about Him? Brian began to practice those principles of application instead of information.

The nursery on Sundays settled in the serving line at Pepperoni's. Mothers would set up their Pack 'n Plays there on the floor and put their kids down during the service.

It was amazing.

But exhausting.

I Need Help

The head pastor of the old church had told Brian one time, "You never know pressure until your office is the last one on the hall." A youth pastor can second-guess, armchair-quarterback, do all of those things.

Now there was no one else. Just Brian. It all began and ended with him.

He learned a few things about church in those first few months, things they don't teach in seminary. In "big church," brokenness isn't valued. It costs time and money and effort and emotion to deal with people in crisis. Broken people are a drain on all the resources.

In a church of four hundred people, for example, a pastor can only get involved when lives are in open crisis (when life circumstances have become so unmanageable that the crisis is laid bare for all to see)—deaths, a kid in jail, affairs, major marital problems, foreclosures, addictions, and more. At any one time, only 5 percent of the congregation will be in open crisis. That's twenty-five people or so. And they take all a pastor's time.

At Phoenix Community, *they were all people in crisis.* Brian had fifty people to deal with. Constantly. While a small church, it felt like twice the size of a big church. And for good reason.

He realized something quickly. *I need help.*

But he barely made any money. Ginney had to go back to work to help support the family when they planted Phoenix Community. They needed outside support to pay the basic expenses of the church. All he had to offer was a small congregation, no money, and long hours dealing with broken, messy people in crisis.

Who would say yes to that?

Exploration

It is important to note that three years after Brian and Ginney began the Phoenix Community of Atlanta, the head pastor of their former church—and close friend—called and apologized for allowing bitterness to creep into his life. Their friendship and love was restored, and they have spoken many times.

When Brian confessed the fear that held him back from saying yes, Charles Stanley asked, "What are you afraid of?"

Perhaps you're in a similar place. You have a dream from God, and it seems impossible. Or dangerous. Or too difficult. You're afraid of what you have to lose or what it will cost.

Second Timothy 1:7 declares, "God has not given us a spirit of fear and timidity, but of power, love, and self-discipline."

Be honest about the fears you're experiencing. What are you afraid of? Acknowledge the fears and give those fears to God. Ask Him what he has to say about those fears.

Take a few moments to write down what God has to say about those fears and the dream he has given you. Then declare them over your life.

_____

_____

_____

_____

CHAPTER 4

Build the Team

B rian asked his good friend Greg Sweatt first.

Greg had been the one who told Brian he wouldn't be able to see his vision at the big church; the two of them had conversations and supported each other as youth pastors over the years. Greg also had his own struggles with the large church culture even while highly successful.

However, Greg dealt with serious family issues while Brian planted the Phoenix Community. Greg's mother had fallen ill, and since his father was in a wheelchair and incapable of taking care of her as she needed, Greg would drive down during the week from northern Georgia to southern Alabama. He worked as the head of a large student ministry when he could.

With all that Greg had going on, as exhausted and stretched as he felt, he told Brian he couldn't.

Brian understood but still needed help. Who else could he ask?

Jeff and Kelly Bagwell were known as rock stars in the student ministry world, working for some of the largest churches in the country, and they served at a church in North Georgia when the Phoenix Community began. But even rock stars want to quit sometimes.

Brian met Jeff and Kelly in seminary through a mutual friend, another youth pastor, and Brian, Jeff, and Kelly grew closer and stayed in contact.

Once Kelly and Jeff moved into North Georgia, their friendship deepened. Jeff spoke for Brian over the years at things like Disciple Now and ski retreats.

While Brian was still at his former church and thinking of creative ways to do the Phoenix Community vision within that organization, he and others from the discovery team went to a church planter's conference at Jeff and Kelly's church in the fall of 2006. Once Brian stepped out and planted the Phoenix Community the next year, he went to the same conference as an independent church planter who needed help with this new experiment.

Jeff was burning out, wearing out, and breaking down. He led an amazing ministry at a large church with great leaders under him, but he was ready to quit.

A Changing Paradigm

Bigger, better was the way. Growing numbers dominated the training in every sense. How could they get more kids? How could the student ministry grow?

By the time Brian talked to Jeff in the fall of 2007, Jeff had already been pushing for changes outside the norm of what was accepted as youth ministry. He asked the question, "Why are we still doing the seventies and eighties model of youth ministry?"

His vision for change began at a church in Gainesville, Georgia, where he started reaching out to different people groups other than white kids. He sought to connect with the growing demographics in the city—African American and Hispanic, specifically. Jeff was already relationship-driven in his outreach, working with the Gainesville High School football team, and he plugged into the community.

Kids from the high school would come to youth events but did not attend on Sundays because they saw it as the "white church." A sign of things to come, Jeff was already reaching out to the broken and marginalized in his community, the hurting and misfits rejected by others, kids that smoked in the parking lot on Wednesday nights. Those kids ruffled the skirts of a few "traditionally minded" members.

And when certain people complain at those kinds of churches, the youth pastor gets pushed out.

Jeff and Kelly left that church and thought they were done with ministry. But a smaller Baptist church in the area needed an interim student minister and offered them a position. The welcoming, friendly atmosphere at that small church showed Jeff and Kelly that they weren't released from the call to serve in ministry. After conversations with the smaller church revealed it wasn't a long-term solution to Jeff's need for employment, he applied and got another position at a larger church.

Within a few months, Jeff found his vision in conflict with leadership again. Feeling that the solution for transformation of the students was a thriving community environment, he wanted to take time to build a leadership team of staff and volunteers. Jeff wanted a community around kids that empowered and inspired the kids, and they would invite their friends to something they felt ownership in. This model seemed to Jeff to be discipleship and evangelism in balance for the best long-term solution.

Leadership didn't agree. The head pastor wanted numbers, more concerned with salvations and baptisms on spreadsheets instead of discipleship and spiritual growth.

The head pastor ran the church like a business, constantly asking how Jeff would bring kids in and pushing for more events. Jeff's philosophy of growth was that if they built an amazing community with support, the growth would come from kids inviting friends because they felt empowered and inspired. He believed in quality over quantity. But that didn't seem to be how the head pastor felt.

The conflict and tension of these diverging visions became clearer and clearer to Jeff, and in a meeting the fall of 2007 with the head pastor, they agreed to part ways. Jeff would have a short time to find something else, but his time at the church was over.

That was two weeks before the church planter's conference that his friend Brian attended.

Jeff was convinced this time, though, that he was done with ministry. Feeling numb, like a failure, he was hurt and rejected time and again. This was it. Maybe he wasn't cut out for this ministry thing. He would just get a job and work to support his family.

Brian Holland sat across from his friend, who was hurting and empty, and he asked Jeff to come and help him at the Phoenix

Community of Atlanta. The position didn't come with much money, only a different way of doing church. Brian couldn't think of anyone more perfect to minister to the marginalized and the broken.

Brokenness Just Is

Brokenness is no respecter of age, race, gender, nationality, or socio-economic status. Brokenness visits anyone and everyone. It just is.

Jeff and Kelly had a heart for the broken and the misfits because of their own story.

While beginning in ministry—Jeff with students and Kelly in pastoral care—and all the potential and excitement that went with it, they became pregnant and had twin boys. Over time, they noticed some issues, minor at first and then more pronounced. Soon the twins were both diagnosed with autism.

It is hard to be a rock star, full-time minister with twin autistic sons. With the "bigger, better" model, the demands took their toll on the family. The term "special needs" doesn't cover the amount of care Jeff and Kelly's sons require. No church could figure out and reconcile the tension between full-time ministry pressures and sensitivity to their family dynamic.

Brian witnessed the struggle firsthand. Jeff spoke at a ski retreat for Brian and thought it would be great for the boys to come and have fun. But one of the twins hated the snow, the sun's bright reflection, hot clothes, boots squeezing his feet, and other forms of stimulation. He didn't enjoy it at all.

To be fair, no one was an expert on how to handle the situations that arose. The twins were autistic before the problems in ministry, and Kelly and Jeff were learning as they went. The boys were only in kindergarten, and everyone was doing their best to try and figure out their needs.

As friends and over the conversations at those church-planting conferences, Jeff knew Brian's vision for the church. It interested him. But then Kelly needed to be convinced.

Brian met with Jeff and Kelly over lunch and listened as Kelly had question after question. How would this work? She had experienced the upheaval of one church experience after another, being hurt over and over again, and as a wife she had watched her husband be rejected for his passion and approach to ministry.

She had also seen her sons misunderstood and ostracized by people in the church and felt protective of them too. She knew they couldn't make it through any more of that.

Those were the big-idea questions. Then came the details of money and numbers and how to make this sustainable and stable for a family with twin special-needs sons.

Brian was as comforting as he could be, but he honestly had very few answers. Phoenix Community was only a couple months old, and he and Ginney were the only example he had to go by. This grand experiment had just begun, and he was still figuring it out too.

Maybe they could figure it out together.

God provided a teaching job for Kelly that gave them benefits, and the Bagwells took this as a sign of provision from God. After much prayer and deliberation, Kelly and Jeff said yes and joined the Phoenix Community of Atlanta.

Forward Together

The vision of the Phoenix Community of Atlanta was for the broken, the hurting, the marginalized, the addicted, the rejected.

If Phoenix Community couldn't value rock star pastors who were also parents of twin special-needs sons and work through that, then what was their vision worth?

Phoenix Community started shifting the paradigm; however, they seemed to be stumbling along in the process.

Considering the standard in ministry at the time, Brian and Jeff should have been looking at bigger and bigger ministries, perhaps head pastor positions, climbing the "ministry ladder."

Another common but tragic option for pastors is to burn out and check out to get jobs other than ministry, as Jeff almost did, for the sake of their families.

The bigger-better model required the work take priority over everything, even family, and pastors often invest all their time, energy, and passion into the work and leave their families behind. Years pass and families wind up in shambles and marriages in divorce. Then those pastors are fired for a failed marriage or kids in serious trouble—an even more tragic reality.

The bigger-better model is a no-win situation for many pastors.

Brian and Jeff stepped out in a serious departure from the common paths: go small, go where the need is greatest, reach out to the people Jesus would have reached out to, the "prostitutes and tax collectors" that would enter the kingdom before the religious and socially accepted or worldly successful (Matthew 21:31).

They had to shake loose from the previous paradigm, get past the ministry box in that time, blow it all up, and do it differently.

The ultimate goal was not to start a new kind of church, though. The goal was to reach people, the addicted and abused like Brian had been before he committed to follow Jesus, the broken and exhausted like Jeff and Kelly with twin autistic sons and nowhere to fit. That necessitated a new kind of church.

In his previous church before Phoenix Community, Brian watched as the pastor and staff made the decision to compete for the 11 percent already attending church instead of the 89 percent in the community not going to church at all. It broke his heart.

Brian and Jeff knew they needed a different kind of church and a different attitude toward church to reach those people. The necessity bred the creativity.

Keeping his family a priority was part of the decision for Jeff Bagwell. Head pastors kept demanding that the church be his priority over family, and he had to make a decision. Was he going to be a dad and husband first and be seen as less in the ministry world? Or would he be a pastor first and lose his family? Jeff made his decision and feels lucky today that he did.

The Numbers Start to Work

Brian may not have had the answers at the time, but the answers began to present themselves. Saying yes to God opened doors in relationships with Jeff Bagwell and his family.

Jeff's vision may have been in conflict with his former head pastor, but other people on staff believed in him and what he was doing.

They also pushed back against the head pastor's focus on numbers. One of those on staff headed up the church-planting program and was in the middle of trying to build the church-planting network. When Jeff told him of the move to Phoenix Community of Atlanta, the pastor got the church to support the Bagwell family at half salary for the first year, which was an amazing blessing to Jeff and the Phoenix Community of Atlanta.

The support for the church plant also took attention off Jeff leaving the bigger church out of conflict and made for a more peaceful exit.

Brian gave Jeff the permission to put his family first. The first Sunday Jeff came to Phoenix Community as a pastor was also the first Sunday he had ridden with his family to church. Ever. And for the next eight years, Jeff and Kelly had that time with their boys in the morning and over long car rides to build relationship and spend time together, which was invaluable to them.

The church continued forward into 2008 with great leadership and creative solutions at Pepperoni's in Duluth. Phoenix Community showed they could bring in a burned-out, misfit leader into the family.

And they were about to bring in another.

Exploration

Brian Holland often says, "You know you're onto something when those closest to you begin to dream the dream God has dreamed in you."

For Brian, it began that day in Brunswick, Georgia, with Ginney and continued when people actually showed up for the church at Pepperoni's. Brian and Ginney's parents began writing checks and supporting the church.

These are signs that others are dreaming the dream God has dreamed in you. Yes, we can do it alone, but that is often not how God desires it. God desires relationship and community. Even Jesus had a group of loyal disciples and friends, like Mary, Martha, and Lazarus, that ministered with him (Matthew 20:17–19; Luke 10:38–42). Paul had Luke and Timothy (Philippians 2:19–23).

Who are the people dreaming God's dream with you? Are the people closest to you affirming that dream?

Have you shared it with them? With anyone?

Who is ready to take the leap with you?

Take a moment to prayerfully consider and write out a list of people with whom you should share the dream God has dreamed in you. Pray for the people on that list and how you should approach them.

_____

_____

_____

_____

_____

_____

_____

_____

_____

_____

_____

_____

_____

_____

CHAPTER 5
Life Is about Relationships

In the spring of 2007, while Brian was still trying to fit his vision into the big church model, Greg Sweatt put together a massive event to bring kids to his church down the road in Dacula, Georgia. There was a popular band, inflatable games, free food, and more. The main attraction of the event was a tricked-out truck giveaway. Fifteen random tickets got a key, and those fifteen teens tried to start the truck. One lucky winner would have the working key. A stunt driver did tricks on a motorcycle, amazed the kids, and gave his testimony.

Seven thousand kids showed up, and hundreds responded to the speaker's invitation to follow Christ that night. It was the biggest, most successful event they had ever done, and Greg—the student minister—was in charge of it all.

The head pastor came to Greg during the frenetic culmination of the event and asked how many kids they had at the event.

Greg answered, "A lot."

The head pastor then asked the question, "What are you going to do next year?"

The question stunned Greg, and the timing floored him. He froze, speechless. How was he going to beat it? How was it going to be better next year?

At this point, Greg realized he could no longer do the "bigger, better" model. In a moment of his greatest success according to that standard, it wasn't good enough. It would never be good enough.

No surprise, then, that when his friend and fellow student pastor, Brian Holland, spoke with him about this new ministry idea he had, the Phoenix Community of Atlanta, Greg told him, "You might as well go on and start your church."

Greg also had a heart for the misfit kids. When he pastored in nearby Lilburn, Georgia, he drew kids like skaters with a portable skate park. Those misfit kids smoked in the parking lot (sound familiar?) and upset some of the parents at that church, despite his success getting kids saved and baptized.

He thought moving up to Dacula would be a better fit, a more rural setting, but as time went on, the area grew; the church found itself in the middle of minorities moving in. Greg had heard another well-known pastor, who also moved his church up to Dacula, make the shocking comment that he wished he had moved the building one exit further, where the money was.

The people moving out to Dacula were the same crowd as the ones from Lilburn, so this didn't bother Greg. While at the church in Dacula, they were seeing kids saved and baptized, but it was never enough. The leaders wanted new programs to bring people in, pressuring pastors, but those same leaders wouldn't allow the old programs to end. Why? Quitting old programs would offend someone, so the level of work and programming at the church would become unmanageable.

During that time in 2007, newer megachurches appeared in the area, churches founded on a semi-nondenominational image with the rise of contemporary music. The younger people went to these new contemporary churches, and it became more difficult to fill a 3,500-seat sanctuary twice on a Sunday at Greg's church.

The pressure built, and it appeared impossible to keep up.

For Greg, the pressure was compounded by his mother's illness and the constant travel to take care of his mother and father.

When Greg's mother died in October 2007, his pastor called and asked how he could pray for Greg. It was the first time in the years he worked in Dacula that anything like that had ever happened.

That conversation with his head pastor was the final confirmation that it was time for Greg to leave the church ... and possibly ministry altogether.

Greg shared his decision with the student ministry staff under him in February 2008. He felt responsible for the final event of the school year, Disciple Now, so he didn't quit yet. He worked through March for the event, getting a big-name speaker and making sure his staff all had what they needed to do an amazing job. Thousands of kids showed up again, and eighty missions projects were supported.

On the Monday after the event, the beginning of April, Greg walked into the head pastor's office and turned in his resignation. Tired emotionally and physically, he explained he couldn't do it anymore.

What was he going to do?

He didn't know. But he knew a church he could hang with.

Taking Time

When Greg and his wife Julie began attending Phoenix Community of Atlanta, Jeff had just come on board a few months earlier, and money was tight. Brian looked at his friend and said, "I don't have anything to offer you."

"That's good," Greg said. "Because if you did, you'd require something of me. I don't have anything left to give."

He needed time to heal and grieve. The death of his mother and the lost dream of a career in ministry left Greg wondering what life was all about. What really mattered?

No longer a pastor, Greg needed a way to make money and pay the bills.

One of Greg's former students from Lilburn had gone on to Piedmont College in Demorest, Georgia, on a baseball scholarship. The college athlete also started mowing lawns to help pay for school. After graduation, the baseball player started teaching at South Gwinnett High School in Snellville with the special education department. But he had built a decent lawn mowing business, more than he could handle now that he taught full time.

There were a few customers in Greg's area, and he asked if Greg would like to cut some lawns for extra money.

Never one to shy away from work and opportunity, Greg agreed. He went to Home Depot and got some cheap lawn equipment like an edger and trimmer. Realizing it was good money, Greg went on to put a sign and phone number on his truck for lawn care.

Adding landscaping for rental properties, he bought more equipment and expanded his skills and customer base. Greg began building a lawn care business of his own from those first few clients. The business not only paid Greg's bills but offered employment opportunities for people in the church, even pastors like Jeff and later Wes Patterson.

What did Julie think about this crazy new Phoenix Church? On the one hand, she always supported Greg's decisions and career paths, and Greg felt as though he had dragged her through life one way or another. Julie had always been an amazing supporter.

But she was tired of the larger churches too. Pastors' wives see the hurt and the wounds, and she had taken many of the issues personally.

It was a difficult transition on the other hand. In a bigger church, a person can hide easily, even the wife of a pastor. At Phoenix, with a smaller number of people, more community based and relational, there was nowhere to hide.

Healing takes time, but God is present and gentle in the process. God is a tender Father.

Six months after his resignation from the church in Dacula, Greg was driving to see a member of the Phoenix church who had been in a wreck, and in that time alone on the drive he wrestled with life and the future. He told God, "I'll do anything."

God said, *Do you trust Me?*

Greg didn't say anything in response at first.

God asked again, *Do you trust Me?*

Greg told God that *yes*, he did.

What If It Were Twenty Churches?

Brian's original vision for the Phoenix Community of Atlanta was a merge-ramp church, a way for people to ultimately find their way into the "big church" from the smaller ministry. His focus would be on the 89 percent of people in the community who were either unchurched or broken and wounded and felt intimidated by the religious, neotraditional model. The initial Phoenix Community idea would address that.

When Brian's former head pastor rejected that model, a new vision emerged. What if this is church? What if the relational, vulnerable, real, and simple approach was the church? What if less programs and more community and intimacy between members was the model for Phoenix Community?

Over the first few months, Greg got more involved as a pastor and leader. His daughter started helping with the kids ministry and helped mentor Brian's daughter Emily.

Greg's questions drove his involvement. What are we doing that matters? What is important? What is making an impact? What if there's something greater than getting seven thousand kids to an event? That is cool, but the numbers alone aren't what it's about.

It is about relationships. It is about working and ministering with families, with friends, with a community of people you love. The rest is just details.

Brian says the Christian journey is not a marathon where you start at this one point and get as far away from the beginning as possible. The Christian life is more like the rings of a freshly cut tree. The genesis moment is always central and essential, and we expand from that point to grow and impact others.

With two pastors added, an important pattern continued. For Brian, Jeff, and now Greg, they ministered to the broken because they understood the pain and wounds of being broken, tired, feeling empty and done. The church ministered to them as well. They were on this journey together as pastors and congregation.

They also fell into their roles, with Brian teaching half of the time on Sundays, and all three leading small groups.

Another initial idea was that Phoenix Community would grow larger and larger. Since the vision of the church was a smaller number of people to better facilitate community and loving the broken in relationship, their goal as they grew was to plant more churches with Phoenix Community principles instead of growing one large one.

Greg challenged the limited thinking of an ever-growing single church in a conversation with Brian. With elbows propped on the bed of Greg's truck, they talked in Greg's driveway, as friends do, and Greg said, "What if it's twenty churches?"

What if it's not one church or two churches? Or even a handful of churches? What if it's twenty around the Atlanta area?

Why not?

How would they fund such an operation?

Not with money from the broken, assuredly. The "poor widow" might give all she's got, but that's two pennies for the support of the pastors and planting more churches. Not a great plan, especially as the financial markets in the US began showing signs of a downward turn.

At the moment, the solution didn't seem complicated. *What if we start a business?*

Okay. But what kind of business?

Clarifying the Vision

Like most things, an idea doesn't come together all at once.

At a leadership meeting around a ping-pong table at the home of one of the founding families of the church, one of the leaders suggested that Phoenix Community be a "marketplace church." What would it look like if they had a business that helped the church engage the community while also providing employment?

They looked into buying an old Atlanta Bread Company location that could be a business during the week and a place for the church to meet on Sunday morning. A café? A coffee shop?

The marketplace church model appealed to Brian. He took business classes in college and university that interested him as much as the theology and ministry classes had. The Atlanta Bread Company option didn't work, but they began brainstorming other solutions.

Coffee was not the first choice, however.

Brian considered the future of alternative fuels, especially the possibility of converting used cooking oil, especially oil from nuts, to make biodiesel. The technology was so new at the time, there could be some opportunity to use french fry peanut oil for that project. Especially from Chick-fil-A.

The Holland family had gone to church with the Cathy family, the founders of Chick-fil-A, and Dan and Truett Cathy had been Brian's Sunday school teachers.

What if they bought the peanut oil from Chick-fil-A? Unfortunately, two weeks before Brian met with the company to do so, they had given the contract to another biodiesel company.

Continuing to brainstorm, they thought about the things that gather people. Phoenix Community was about relationships and community, and if they were to be a marketplace church, what sort of things brought people together?

Cigars. Men who got together to smoke a cigar with one another were making a social contract to have conversation and relationship.

Beer. People got together for all kinds of events with beer. Having a beer with someone communicated a connection and relationship.

With the context of being former Baptist-seminary trained ministers, the pastors didn't think cigars or beer would be viewed as the wisest of choices.

Looking down at the table, they noticed the cups in front of them.

Coffee. Coffee brings people together. Men and women both love it. Coffee shop-type churches were beginning to pop up in certain parts of the country, a third-space solution during the week to engage the community and a spot to have worship on Sunday morning.

Brian, Greg, and Jeff met at coffee shops all the time to have conversations, and those conversations would spill over into making connections at the next table as people asked questions about topics they struggled with, that even the pastors struggled with.

Coffee. That was it. They would start a coffee shop.

The next step was to find funding to start one.

Then the greatest financial crisis since the Great Depression hit.

Exploration

It is often difficult to share hurts, wounds, and weaknesses with others, especially for pastors. We take pictures of the good times, the successes, and the smiles. Social media compounds the good life we wish to show the rest of the world.

For Brian, Jeff, and Greg, they learned to share their struggles and brokenness with each other, bonding as brothers. The Holland, Bagwell, and Sweatt families also grew close during this formative time, working and living life together.

Even Jesus needed to have friends and partners who ministered to Him through His hard times (Luke 22:28).

Who are those people in your life? Who can you be vulnerable with for strength, encouragement, and accountability? It doesn't need to be a large group (Jesus had less than twelve), but we do need them. Write down each person who fits that description in your life. Then pray and thank God for them.

_____

_____

_____

_____

_____

_____

_____

_____

_____

_____

_____

_____

CHAPTER 6

God Has the Script

Just as other missions organizations raise support, Phoenix Community of Atlanta did the same. With such a small church and the vision to go into the broken and hurting of the city, other churches and individuals saw Phoenix Community as a type of mission and supported them as such.

Brian had people who supported him individually, notably his parents, who gave generously every month.

Greg's lawn care business paid his bills and helped others with employment.

Jeff had others who supported him besides his former church, and he coached football at Lakeview Academy.

Their wives—Ginney, Julie, and Kelly—all worked full time to help pay bills and provide health insurance for their families.

Money was tight at the church, but they were seeing God work. They knew they were in His will and doing something important. Something that mattered.

The church grew in numbers. More and more of the broken and wounded found a home at Phoenix Community, which continued to grow in need but not in money. People in pain or addicted or in crisis find it difficult to give.

The church didn't have much turnover, but a few members who were giving financially left for other places.

And when the recession hit in the summer of 2008, churches desperate to make it through the financial hard times revisited their giving. All but two churches withdrew their support to Phoenix Community.

What had been a tight financial situation before now became a crisis even for the pastors. And God had them in the middle of starting a business.

It's in the Bean

By the fall of 2008, every month included a crisis point. With less money and more need, the paychecks for the pastors averaged far below the poverty line.

At the end of each month, Phoenix would pay the expenses first—rent and utilities. Then whatever they had left over was split three ways for the pastors. Brian would go to Chris Dawkins to get the checks for the month. Chris was one of the leaders of the church, a successful businessman, and led worship on Sunday at Phoenix Community. He also ran the books for the church.

Chris would put the numbers into a spreadsheet and come out with the amounts for each pastor. Often he and Brian would both weep at the numbers on the checks.

That fall, Brian drove from Chris's office to deliver the paychecks, frustrated and discouraged, knowing there had to be a better way. He asked God, "What do You want me to do?"

Brian passed Waffle House. "You want me to work at Waffle House?"

No, God answered. *Because you'll work all night, do church all day, and never see your family.*

Home Depot was also on the route. "Okay, God. You want me to work at Home Depot?"

God said, *no. You'll work all day, do church all night, and ignore your family.*

Brian repeated the question eerily similar to Greg's on a separate drive. "What do You want me to do?"

An idea came to Brian's mind, and then God spoke. Brian pulled into the Home Depot parking lot and heard God speak.

It's not in the coffee shop; it's in the coffee bean.

The money, Brian understood. They had been focused on opening a coffee shop and working through that to make money and hire people. But coffee shops notoriously failed. Sometimes banks wouldn't give loans to coffee shops because of their track record.

But what about selling the bean? Was there was more money in that? You're going to have to explain that to me, Brian thought.

Then God gave him a picture. Brian pulled out a napkin, found a pen, and drew the picture.

It started with vague shapes that represented Georgia and Florida. He drew a star in the North Georgia area to represent Atlanta. There was a V for Venezuela, the country Brian thought had coffee, possibly. Next came a coffee tree, which didn't look much like a coffee tree, more like an oak tree. The ideas were there. Three pictures. What did it mean?

He drove to Greg's house in Dacula, told Greg the story of how God spoke to him, and showed him the napkin. "What is it?" Greg asked.

"I don't know," Brian said. "I was hoping you could tell me." He took the napkin, studied it, turning it around 360 degrees.

Then Greg took the pen and drew arrows connecting the three images—Venezuela, Atlanta, and the coffee tree.

Greg explained. "What if we used coffee from Central America and sell it to churches, and that became our revenue stream to plant more churches?"

It was becoming more and more clear.

Drink This Coffee Black

Meeting with a friend in coffee was the first time the Phoenix Community pastors had high-quality specialty coffee. The friend did a tasting with them and educated them on topics like flavor profiles and some basics the pastors didn't know.

As a man used to putting powdered creamer in his coffee, the flavor amazed Greg, and he said, "I can drink this black."

And so the Phoenix Community coffee company—Phoenix Roasters—began bagging coffee in the fall of 2008. They would buy it roasted from their coffee friend, bag it, label it, and then sell it to churches or groups when they could.

The margin from roasted bean to the customer was thin, however. Even when they were making some money, it wasn't much.

In a leadership meeting, Greg made the definitive statement. "We're never going to make money selling other people's coffee."

"Well, what's the alternative?" they asked Greg.

"We need to roast our own coffee," he responded.

To roast their own coffee, they needed a roaster.

The leadership team consisted of the three pastors, an engineer, a salesman, an IT manager, and a construction supervisor. No matter how fast they were learning about coffee, they still didn't know much. So when Greg made that statement, it made him the expert in the room. The old leadership principle of telling the guy with the genius idea that it's now his job, Brian and Jeff asked, "What kind of roaster do we need?"

Greg may have been the "resident expert," but he didn't have the answer to that question.

He went away and did some research over the next few weeks and found the solution. The Probat, twelve-kilogram, hand-built German engineered roaster made in 1996 that roasted seventy-five to one hundred pounds an hour. Only one thousand of them existed. But they were renowned for being sturdy and easy to fix if broken.

That sounded great to everyone. How much did it cost?

The number was $27,000, but that didn't matter. They didn't have the money to even come close. Should they borrow money? The leadership team batted around some solutions, but Chris Dawkins and the other leaders suggested one radical idea.

Pray. They didn't have the money, but they could pray. The foundation of the church was a word from Charles Stanley that said, "Don't you know God takes responsibility for all the consequences of a heart that's devoted to Him?"

Did they?

They knew the business and the vision was the right direction, but they didn't know how God was going to do it. They all agreed. Yes. The correct solution was to pray.

They just didn't know it was going to take so long.

Growth and Relationships

Over the next year, they continued to pray, and while they didn't get a roaster, that didn't mean God wasn't working.

That time was spent building relationships in the church and among the three pastors. Brian, Greg, and Jeff would meet at the YMCA and work out together. They met at Starbucks and talked, meeting people and starting meaningful conversations.

Jeff continued to connect with people in Gainesville—people like the owner of Little Italy's Pizza and pastors and others at Lakewood Baptist Church. Jeff's purpose was to love and connect, but those relationships also helped when he planted a Phoenix Community church in Gainesville years later.

The pastors started and maintained an important relationship with Joe Wingo at Angel Food Ministries in Monroe, Georgia. Every month, a couple of the pastors and a few dedicated church volunteers would go at 4:00 a.m. and pick up food boxes for the poor and needy prepared at Angel Food, which they handed out on Saturday mornings in Duluth. Members of Phoenix Community would help pass out boxes and talk to others. That was one way the church met the hurting and the needy in the community. The church grew and gathered more people over time.

Each time they saw Joe or hung around him, they saw the impact his giving and generosity had on others. Dozens of people would line up to talk to him and share testimonies with anyone who would listen of how he had helped them with rent, an electric bill, or feeding the family during a crisis. Some shared stories of appliances and even a car that Joe and his wife had purchased for them. Joe always had money in a pocket that he would give away to people when hearing their stories of need.

The pastors were needy too. Swallowing their pride, they would pick up food for themselves, and the pastors never left without boxes of steak and chicken. Joe would tell Greg, who usually picked up the boxes, to take the food to Jeff and the boys.

One Christmas, in fact, Brian and the pastors had the idea of giving Joe packets of coffee to put into the boxes for those in need. The three of them sat in his office.

Joe stared at them. "You don't have anything for your families for Christmas, do you?"

"No, sir," Brian told them.

"I'll be right back," he announced and left the office. He returned with his and his wife's checkbook.

The man wrote out three $500 checks and handed one to each of the pastors.

"Don't give this to anyone else," Joe said. "I know you three. I know you'll find someone else to give it to. This is to buy something for your wives." All four of them wept at the kindness and generosity.

The Phoenix pastors were able to have a Christmas that year, and they never forgot his kindness.

Years later, Joe dealt with criminal activity and corruption in his organization and family. Joe had to spend some time in prison. Greg had kept in touch with Joe, and Phoenix Community was able to give money to his family and help them through a hard time as well.

God Has the Script

Long before Phoenix Community, Brian and Greg were part of a group of student pastors in the north Georgia area. They met for years to encourage one another, talk, share issues, and pray for each other. These pastors would meet and eat and live life together. Deep relationships were built.

At one time the group swelled to twenty student pastors, but nine of them were the core for seven years. They went on trips and spoke at each other's camps.

The pastors possessed years of experience, and Greg said, "Lack of friends and finances, that's what closes churches." They might not have had much money, but they wanted to have close friendships and relationships. They knew they needed them.

When Brian, Greg, and Jeff began talking about church planting, Greg wanted the pastors to live like that. The Monday morning meetings developed from that idea, where all the pastors would develop messages together and pray. A core leadership principle developed—no matter how large the Phoenix Community pastor group becomes, this time of prayer and gathering is required.

It was an isolating time for them, learning what it meant to continue to shift the paradigm from "bigger, better" to relationships and community.

They tried to go to Catalyst Leadership Conference in Atlanta and learn, but the models were still testimonies from churches and leaders with larger and larger numbers. After one day at Catalyst, Jeff felt like such a failure that he didn't go back.

It wasn't Catalyst's fault, however. Brian, Greg, and Jeff needed to change the conversation and distance themselves from that mindset of ministry to move forward into what God had called them to do specifically. Much of what those conferences offered was a script of how to replicate those successes, but for Phoenix Community, their measures for success looked different. No one in those conference circles was stepping out to do what the three Phoenix pastors were attempting, so the comparisons became a trap for them.

It was a lonely time. Brian remembers feeling like Kevin Costner in the movie *Dances with Wolves*—out in the wilderness and alone.

The result was they huddled and prayed and followed God.

A large portion of their story looked like stumbling, and still does, because they believe themselves successful because of one thing—saying yes.

It looks like stumbling and trying to find their way. They didn't set out to be pioneers but rather to reach the broken. They didn't know anyone in the larger church culture who had a script for what God had called them to do.

God has the script. That's not stumbling. That's saying yes to God and trusting Him for the results. He had shown up to do miracles before. He would again.

Wouldn't He?

Exploration

Saying yes to God leads to experiencing more intimacy and favor with God. Brian calls this the Favor Cycle, and it is the process of taking God's favor and grace to obey and follow Him. That obedience leads to more favor to influence and impact others for the kingdom.

Stage one of the Favor Cycle begins with core truths about who God is. God is good, and all good things come from him (Exodus 34:6; James 1:17). His grace is unmerited (Galatians 3:18). For the followers of Jesus, the Father's favor is unlimited.

What does it mean that God's favor is unlimited? Jesus said that God gave Him the "Spirit without limit" (John 3:34). When praying to the Father for the disciples, Jesus said, "As you sent me into the world, I am sending them into the world" (John 17:18). He promised the gift and counselor of the Holy Spirit in the same discourse.

The heart of God is to share all things with us out of love—grace we didn't earn and an unlimited amount of favor available to us.

Take time now to praise God for who He is, what He's done, what He's doing, and the good He will do in the future. Write down three specific things God has done in your life you can praise Him for.

_____

_____

_____

_____

_____

_____

_____

_____

_____

_____

CHAPTER 7

What Are the Chances?

Trusting God, praying, and waiting for Him to move sounds very spiritual.

But it involves hard times and the kinds of seasons that make people want to quit.

Other ministers and friends saw how God was working at Phoenix Community and heard the stories of both the church and the coffee. Those stories would inspire others as something unique and refreshing.

That was ironic to Brian, Jeff, and Greg.

The first major church Brian wanted to make a coffee partner was in nearby Norcross, Georgia. They already served coffee on Sunday mornings. He met with the pastor and only asked that they switch their coffee to Phoenix Roasters and start supporting church planting and ministry to the hurting and broken.

The church in Norcross said they didn't want to be the first. They wanted to wait until others came on board. Brian knew that meant no.

After selling their first few pounds of coffee from their friend in coffee, Phoenix Roasters started buying from Jittery Joe's and, with their generous permission, relabeling to sell—not a long-term solution at all. But what could they do? They needed a roaster. Something had to happen soon.

In April 2009, Greg bought a house in Buford. A small, older brick house on an acre, Greg saw the possibilities. It had room to add on and still have a great back yard. He sold his nice house in Dacula and purchased the new one with his dad's help.

His wife Julie wasn't so sure. It had sat empty for years and needed a lot of work. Greg looked at his skeptical wife and said, "You gotta picture it."

Greg spent months tearing down sheetrock, pulling nails, doing work that was way bigger than he had expected. The reality hit him. *What have I done?* It was emotional and cathartic work.

He gave his children decisions to make, knowing it would give them ownership in the final product. Julie made most of the choices regarding the decorations. Eventually he moved into an amazing house in Buford.

For month after month, the Phoenix pastors barely hung on. They would minister and work only to go home and wonder if they could come back the next day. Brian remembers that time as one where if any one of them had said, "Yeah, I'm quitting," that the others would say, "Yep. You're right. This is over." They wouldn't have survived.

However much they might have thought it, none of them said it. They kept showing up.

And God showed up too. Just like Greg took an old house and restored it into something new, God was building something behind the scenes.

You the Coffee Pastor?

On a freezing cold afternoon in Suwanee, Georgia, Brian stood at the fence at a lacrosse practice where his son, Duke, played. Mark Adams, a volunteer at Sugar Hill Methodist Church with WyldLife, a middle school ministry in public schools, came up to Brian. Mark's son played on Duke's team. He said, "Hey, I know you. You're the coffee pastor, right?"

It was February 2010. And while Phoenix Roasters was selling coffee, mostly through helping churches fundraise, Brian didn't feel qualified to claim he was the coffee pastor. But he did.

Mark explained to Brian that there was a ministry friend he had to meet.

Who? A missionary with Young Life, a high school ministry in public schools associated with WyldLife, who had something to do with coffee. Mark wasn't sure what the story was exactly, but he wanted to make the connection. The missionary's name was Hunter Lambeth.

Brian thought, *great, this Hunter guy is probably killing it with coffee and probably knows everything about the business. I don't feel like I know anything, and we're dying over here.*

Brian politely agreed to meet with Hunter, but didn't call him. Why would he meet with a missionary who would make Brian feel like a failure? With strapped finances and a floundering coffee idea, he already felt like failure enough.

But Mark Adams wouldn't let the idea go. He emailed Brian and Hunter and introduced them. Now there was no excuse not to meet, he told them.

It took Brian longer still to respond, but he eventually agreed to meet Hunter at a nearby Starbucks in April.

Hunter began with his story. He was going to use coffee from Nicaragua as a revenue stream for Young Life, but that fell apart.

Hunter had connected with the Mejia family in Matagalpa, Nicaragua, close to a Young Life camp. When the government intervened in an attempt to grab control of the country's resources, including coffee, they killed the patriarch of the family, and the project was scrapped. Hunter was left with an investment in a business and family he didn't want to give up on. The Mejia family trusted him, so they shipped the coffee equipment to Hunter to protect their investments. The equipment was currently sitting in storage in Atlanta.

After telling his story, he asked Brian what Phoenix Community did with coffee.

Brian explained the vision. "We want to be a church that uses coffee-roasting revenue to support church planting."

"That's cool," Hunter said. "Do you have a roaster?"

Brian hung his head, feeling exposed as the failure he feared he was. "No. We've been praying for one."

"I've got a roaster," Hunter said.

Brian winced. "Well, we've been praying for this specific one. It's a Probat L12, hand-built German roaster made in 1996."

Hunter shrugged. "I don't know what kind it is, but it's in a storage facility about five miles from here. Let's go look at it."

They met at the storage facility nearby, got out of the car, and went to the space. Hunter lifted the roll-up door.

Sitting in the storage space was a Probat L12, hand-built German-engineered roaster made in 1996.

Brian couldn't believe it. The exact one they started praying for in the fall of 2008. It was now April 2010. "We've been praying for this roaster for eighteen months."

"I put this roaster in here eighteen months ago," Hunter said.

Brian took pictures on his phone and sent them to Greg and others. *You'll never guess what I'm standing in front of,* he told them.

Relationship First

Hunter didn't have the authority to give Phoenix Roasters the roaster. The Mejia family owned it. At the time, Hunter organized details for Young Life international trips while waiting to go to his next assignment in Israel (Phoenix Community now supports Hunter in Israel).

Brian and Hunter went down to Nicaragua to meet with Mario Mejia and ask about the roaster in person in July 2010.

Mario picked them up at the airport and drove them out to Matagalpa and their compound. Brian started to bring up the roaster, but Mario put him off. He told Brian not to rush it.

Brian and Hunter went with Mario to several places, including the Young Life farm, even giving Brian a crash course in roasting. Brian tried a few more times to broach the subject through an interpreter. Mario wouldn't have the discussion. At some point, Brian gave up and stopped asking.

For Mario, the relationship came before business. They spent time together for a week.

On the way back to the airport to leave the country, Mario was speeding along the narrow roads when he looked over at Brian. "Didn't you want to talk about the roaster?"

"Oh, yeah," Brian said.

"We prayed about it as a family," Mario said. "You can use the roaster."

A New Place

While they appreciated Phil and their time at Pepperoni's Pizza, they knew they couldn't put a roaster in the pizza place. They started looking for a warehouse space around Duluth.

At the same time, one of the friends of Phoenix passed away from his long and difficult bout with cancer. The Phoenix Community pastors and church had walked with the member through his illness, and upon his death, he left Phoenix Community $10,000. A family friend of the deceased man matched the donation with another $5,000.

With that money, they were able to move into a warehouse space almost across the street from Pepperoni's and buy chairs and supplies. Members of the church were instrumental in helping fix up the warehouse for the roaster and the church. Others came to paint and remodel, knock down and rebuild walls.

They built the roaster room and turned another area into a coffee café. The son of one of the members needed money, and Phoenix hired him to insulate the attic storage area. Phoenix met other people's needs with employment.

The warehouse had a heater, but they would need an air conditioner to hold summer services in Georgia. A friend of Brian's owned an HVAC company and donated a used air conditioner for the warehouse and installed it.

It was a team effort getting from Pepperoni's to the warehouse. They got it all moved in by August 2010, and Brian roasted the first batch of coffee on October 11, 2010. Hunter even came by to help with the first roast since he had been present at Mario Mejia's lesson in Nicaragua.

The church continued to use salad bowls from Pepperoni's for the offering. A coffee barrel became the pulpit.

Right after moving into the warehouse, Phoenix Roasters received an order for twelve thousand fractional packs of coffee for a specialty e-commerce company. Fractional pack is a small one- or two-ounce bag of grounds that makes a pot of coffee. With coffee bought from Young Life, they got to work.

Phoenix knew very little about how to clean and maintain a roaster. Brian had his thirty-minute training from Mario, a new warehouse, and thousands of pounds to roast. He called Andreas van Honk, a German engineer with Probat, the company that built the roaster, and an expert on their machine. The roaster came with a manual, but it was hard to understand and so basic that it didn't help at all. Brian needed further help.

In conversations with Andreas, he asked Brian, "Have you had your first fire yet?"

Brian scoffed. "No. I'm not going to catch it on fire."

"Sure. Sure. Call me when you have your first fire," Andres said.

In January of the next year, Brian was roasting away when the chaff in the roaster caught fire.

The back panel blew out, and the flames rose up the vent like a rocket about to take off.

A member of the church happened to be there, and she rushed in to connect a hose to a nearby sink, turning the water and spraying everything. Soon Brian was soaked trying to get the hose down into the roaster.

Jeff leapt into the roasting room like an action hero with a fire extinguisher and doused the flames.

Thick smoke was everywhere. They opened the main rolling door to the warehouse to get the smoke out, but it hung in the warehouse. Everyone had to duck and practically crawl to get out of the black-and-gray cloud.

Then the fire department showed up.

With the fire out, they cleaned the roaster as well as they could. It might have been in their minds, but for weeks they swore the coffee had fire extinguisher as one of the flavor nodes.

Brian called Andreas. "Well, I have bad news. I caught the roaster on fire."

Andreas laughed and spoke, drawing out every word. "Good, Brian! Now tell me. What have you learned?"

100 Percent Rule

Years have passed since Brian shook hands with Charles Stanley and heard, "Don't you know that God will take responsibility for all the consequences of a heart that's fully devoted to Him?"

Brian held on to that promise and truth moving forward to start the Phoenix Community of Atlanta, and Jeff and Greg and the other pastors and those who work with Phoenix Community have learned to hold on to that promise as well.

Meeting people like Hunter along the way, Phoenix Community has developed a rule based on a mission trip where Greg saw dozens of examples of saying yes and seeing God show up in response to their obedience. They call it the 100 percent rule.

What are the chances that if you're walking the path God has for you, you'll see Jesus work?

One hundred percent.

With everything from talking with a pizza restaurant owner to getting a roaster after praying for that specific one for eighteen months, the rule has been one truth and proved by experience.

Phoenix Roasters bought their first twelve thousand pounds of raw green beans from Young Life, and that was the first idea that the coffee could do more than help plant churches. It could also support missions directly. The Young Life coffee funded missions and evangelism, raising scholarship money for young people to go to camps and other programs.

Coffee could do more than help support the pastors and plant more churches. It could have an effect on missions around the world.

Just as God led the Phoenix Community pastors to do church differently, he led them step-by-step through how to do coffee differently. Remember, God is more about relationship than the bottom line.

The Young Life coffee ran out over the next year and a half. And when they contacted the Young Life directors for more, the farmers had already sold their crop to someone in California.

Phoenix Coffee got coffee from wherever they could. But they needed a source for their growing coffee company. Something that would support missions. But where? How?

As God tends to do, he used the problem as an opportunity.

Exploration

I visited Niagara Falls years ago, viewing the beautiful and massive amount of water roaring over the gorge—over six million cubic feet of water that drop more than 160 feet every minute. While not unlimited, that's a lot of water.

What if we went to the Falls to collect water and brought only an eight-ounce cup? Or a bucket? Like Elisha and the widow with the oil and vessels, the amount of water we could take away would be dependent upon the vessel we bring to it (2 Kings 4).

In stage two of the Favor Cycle, we learn that while the amount of favor is unlimited, the amount of favor we experience is dependent upon our obedience (Psalm 84:11; Matthew 6:31–33).

Don't confuse the favor of God with worldly wealth or success. Those things may happen, and He promises to provide for our needs, but the favor God bestows is greater revelation of the kingdom of God, more spiritual fruit, more generosity and compassion. In the favor of God, He answers our prayers according to the story He is telling, a redemptive purpose. In obedience, we ask "in [his] name" (John 14:14).

Often we feel God is distant or isn't teaching us anything new, but sometimes He's waiting for us to learn and apply the previous truth He revealed to us (James 1:22; 1 Kings 2:3). A lack of obedience keeps us from experiencing more of God's intimacy and favor. Saying yes is the key that unlocks God's favor in our lives.

Take time to pray for the grace to obey the truths God is teaching you. Ask God, "Are there any truths You've been trying to teach me that I've ignored or refused to obey?"

Write down one thing God is currently asking you to say yes to.

_____

_____

_____

CHAPTER 8
The Circle Expands

Growing up in Alabama, Greg Sweatt learned that anytime a stray dog came to the house, if you pet it and feed it, it's your dog now.

God gave Brian a vision for a church for the broken and hurting, and he didn't only attract a congregation of marginalized people. He gathered pastors that had been rejected or exhausted or both, people worn out from the stress and the unhealthy aspects of the "bigger, better" church world. Stray pastors.

Brian, Jeff, and Greg all had years of relationships with pastors and ministers all over Georgia and the South. Even beyond the student pastor support group that Greg and Brian were a part of, decades or more of ministry at large churches afforded the Phoenix Community pastors connections at all kinds of ministries.

The Phoenix Community pastors knew story after story of pastors finding themselves in an empty, dry place, ready to quit and hang it all up out of exhaustion. Brian and the others could relate to those pastors and leaders.

The Phoenix Community model became known as an alternative choice, or at least helped others see that an alternative choice existed. For those feeling stuck in ministry positions divorced from their passions and gifts, those who cringed and struggled under the weight of a numbers game and misaligned priorities, Phoenix Community proved that there could be another way, a more creative and unique way than the limited options they saw before them.

Heart of a Disciple

Wes Patterson was one of those stray pastors.

He also had a long-standing friendship with Brian, who even helped Wes get hired at a nearby Baptist church in Suwanee, Georgia, as a youth pastor.

Wes didn't have the normal path to ministry. He didn't do the seminary track. Although he grew up in church in Alabama and believed, he hadn't gone through discipleship until college. The discipleship process and experience—being taught how to grow in his relationship with Christ and teach others the same—opened up his eyes and gave his relationship with God a depth he didn't know existed. Discipleship inspired Wes and his wife Becky and opened doors for ministry that led them into youth ministry.

He met Brian in his second year of ministry, and they kept in touch, enjoying their times together, laughing and connecting as leaders who focused on relationship.

Wes's church in Suwanee started buying Phoenix Roasters coffee for fundraising, and he would stop by the warehouse to pick up the coffee and talk. Within those conversations, he heard all the amazing things God was doing within the Phoenix Community church. Lives were being changed and transformed through love and simple dignity and relationship.

The stripped-down, relationship-focused model appealed to Wes as well. His wife Becky would see his eyes light up and hear the passion in his voice when he came home after talking with Brian.

It was ironic, however, that he was inspired during some of the hardest times in Phoenix Community's history. He saw the impact on lives and the community, the unique and creative way God moved, but behind the scenes the pastors still struggled to make ends meet and keep a church and a business running.

While Wes's church had been a huge part of the Suwanee community for decades, they were more traditional, and when a contemporary megachurch built a large satellite campus within minutes of their location, the head pastor spoke with Wes.

It didn't take a prophet to see that the younger crowd in a more traditional church would be attracted to the large, contemporary church. What was Wes going to do? How was Wes going to compete with the mega contemporary church?

"I'm going to keep doing what I'm doing," Wes answered. "I'm on a restricted budget. I can't compete with the big show of that church."

The head pastor asked about Wes's plan for growth.

The youth group had been growing, and Wes explained his plan. "I'm going to disciple about thirty kids, and as they grow, they'll invite friends and become leaders and the group will grow that way."

The head pastor didn't agree, and while Wes had a good relationship with his pastor, he also experienced burnout. He desired a more intimate, discipleship-based model, and he felt he needed more time with his own children, the oldest of which was into the middle school years.

Soon Brian ventured an idea. "What if you came on board with us to help Greg plant a Phoenix Community church in Buford? You could lead worship."

Wes prayed about it, and he talked with Becky.

The money would be less. They'd have to raise support. Becky homeschooled the kids, so she didn't feel like she could get a full-time job. How would they make ends meet? Pay the mortgage? They spoke, and she wept in the laundry room of their house at the frightening reality of what it all meant.

Ultimately, though, the question wasn't one of salary but of obedience. Was God telling them this was what He wanted them to do? If it was, then they had to trust Him with the finances. After more prayer and discussion, they agreed this was God's direction.

They said yes and trusted God with the consequences.

To the credit of the Wes and Becky's relationship with their former pastor, that church committed to support the Pattersons monthly, even through the leanest times of the recession.

The First Phoenix Church Plant

Buford made sense for the first church plant from the main campus in Duluth.

The space in Duluth was full every Sunday, standing room only. Greg, the one who inspired the idea of twenty church plants one day, lived in Buford, as did several of the church members. Wes came on and lived minutes from Buford too. With a teaching pastor and another to lead worship and several families and couples ready and excited for the new venture, Phoenix moved forward with its first church plant.

The pastors searched and found a decent-sized strip mall space with reasonable rent.

The Phoenix Community of Buford opened in October 2012. As meetings began, the pastors met others in the city and brought them into the gathering. Whether old relationships from former churches, people looking for a different kind of church, or the broken and marginalized right down the street, the Buford church started and continued to grow.

They were beginning to see the vision take shape. A coffee company. A roaster. Wes learned what he could from Brian and started roasting green bean.

Church planting. Reaching out to the wounded and hurting.

Both aspects connected for the kingdom.

But they had run out of coffee bean, a fairly necessary element to use the roaster and keep the company going.

The Only One Who Spoke English

The Young Life coffee supply from 2010 ended, and the Mejia family was having problems selling their crop due to conflicts with the government.

The Young Life relationship had been good and opened Phoenix Roasters to the idea of coffee working for the kingdom overseas along with the church planting in the US. But they needed to find another consistent specialty bean that would support missions and evangelism.

Greg's missionary friend, Steve Nolen, had returned from Central and South America around that same time. Steve had connected with the larger church in Dacula, and Greg kept in contact with him over the years.

Steve and his wife Ruth returned from the mission field realizing a difficult truth. Missionaries from Central and South America would be trained in evangelism and other basic ministry skills. These willing and inspired missionaries would get to a foreign country full of potential and promise, but they would end up rarely leaving their house and engaging the culture.

Why? Language acquisition is a constant problem, and it takes certain skills to make friends and participate in the local community. The Nolens developed a program where those missionaries would come to America and be trained in how to learn a language by engaging and learning from the local community. These immersion linguistic learning skills would allow the missionaries to go into any situation and learn a language organically and in relationship.

Steve and Greg talked, and the Nolens invited Greg and Brian to a small conference, an initial meeting to discuss Steve and Ruth's new language training program. People from all over the world would be there, and Steve thought that maybe God would show up.

Brian and Greg prayed before attending the conference, asking God specifically for a contact, a "man of peace" who would help them move forward in their endeavor. Since they didn't want an interruption in coffee supply, what if they owned a farm themselves? Phoenix Roasters could buy a coffee farm in another country and import to America. Who could help them do that? With little to no money?

When they arrived at the meeting, there were thirty or more people, and all of them spoke Spanish. Steve and Ruth Nolen also spoke in Spanish.

Brian and Greg did not speak Spanish.

Unable to understand or communicate with the others, they decided to stay for the free lunch and leave.

As they were leaving during the break, they heard a man speaking English. They thought this must be the man of peace they were looking for since it was the first thing they had understood. They introduced themselves to the man—Perry Walker.

Brian and Greg stood with Perry in the hallway and spoke with him. Perry asked what they wanted to do.

"We want to go down to Central America and buy a coffee farm, start growing the coffee, and import it to roast and sell here in America."

Perry brought out an architect pad and took notes.

When Brian and Greg got done explaining their plan and idea, Perry spoke.

"Let me see if I've got this straight. Your plan is to move to an underdeveloped country, buy their land for cheap, grow their number-one resource, export it cheaply, leaving them in the same condition or worse as when you got there?"

There was a long pause.

It sounded bad when Perry put it like that, but Brian responded, "Um. Not sure when you put it that way, but what else is there?"

Perry began to tell Brian and Greg that there are mission-minded, indigenous farmers all over Latin America. Families that own their own land and grow some of the top specialty coffee in the world. Perry was the pastor to hundreds of indigenous and American missionary pastors in Latin America. He knew many of those farmers.

Brian and Greg had never even considered it.

These farmers, Perry continued, were mission-minded and wanted to do more for the kingdom in their community and country, but companies give them slave wages for the coffee.

What if Phoenix Roasters just bought their coffee at a better price?

What if Phoenix Roasters paid them directly, cutting out the importers, all the middlemen, and imported the coffee from the farmers?

Phoenix Roasters started as a church for the poor, the addicted, and the marginalized, a different idea of church. Could their model of coffee also be unique and different?

The idea Perry planted in their brain was a revolutionary one. They would find indigenous, mission-minded farmers who grew excellent coffee. Phoenix Roasters would pay a better price for the coffee directly to the farmer, and that exchange would transform the communities and countries where the coffee came from.

Of course. It went along with all of the principles God had been teaching them. But where would they get this coffee?

Energized by this new idea, Brian and Greg spoke to Steve Nolen about it. Steve had a friend in Panama City, Panama, and that friend had told Steve about this farming family that grew amazing specialty-grade Arabica coffee and supported forty-seven missionaries.

Forty-seven missionaries.

Steve was going back down to Central America the summer of 2012 for the Business as Mission Conference in Managua, Nicaragua. This would be a great opportunity to try and find those mission-minded farmers. He invited them to come with him to the conference and have opportunities to share about their vision.

When the conference was over, Steve told them they could go to Panama and try to meet these farmers.

It may or may not surprise you, but Brian and Greg said yes.

Exploration

Everyone will experience hard times. Tragedies happen. Whether the normal progress of life or a result of this corrupt world, difficult seasons will be a part of our life.

Jesus promises this: "Here on earth you will have many trials and sorrows." He also adds, "But take heart, because I have overcome the world" (John 16:33).

Stage three of the Favor Cycle is that the size and strength of our foundation is based on our faithfulness and obedience. That foundation will determine how well we weather the storms of life that come to us all.

Jesus teaches the famous parable of the foundations of rock or sand in Matthew 7. It speaks of two men—one who built his life on the rock, the other on the sand. Both heard the words of Jesus. The difference? The one on the rock obeyed the words and survived the storm; the man on the sand didn't obey, and his house collapsed with a "mighty crash" (v. 27).

Walking with God through the storms also deepens intimacy with Christ so that we better realize our dependence upon Him and His comfort and faithfulness.

Take a few minutes to write down examples from when God has seen you through a hard time in the past. Express your need of Him in any storms you are experiencing currently.

_____

_____

_____

_____

_____

_____

_____

_____

_____

_____

_____

_____

_____

_____

_____

_____

_____

_____

_____

CHAPTER 9
Tomato Coffee

Interesting how something as small as a tooth can rearrange plans. One of Brian's wisdom teeth became infected, and the pain was so great, he couldn't lie down to sleep. Just to get some rest, he had to lean his head into a pillow while standing in a corner.

Brian stayed in the US to have dental work while Greg went down to Nicaragua. Morgan Lopes, who was on the Phoenix Roasters team at the time, went with Greg.

Other leaders and ministers from America went on the trip with Steve Nolen to the Business as Mission Conference in Managua. One was the head pastor at a large church where Greg had been trying to sell Phoenix Roasters coffee for a year, but nothing had happened. Greg finally gave up trying.

Greg and Morgan shared a few times over the conference about Phoenix Roasters and their vision for the coffee. By happenstance, Greg would sit next to the pastor of the church in Snellville during other presentations. Never one to shy away from a topic, Greg turned to him and asked, "Why won't you guys buy our coffee?"

The pastor answered that he didn't think the coffee tasted very good. But that led to more discussions and relationship with the church, which did begin buying the coffee later.

After the conference, Greg, Morgan, and Steve made their way to Panama. Brian had the wisdom tooth removed and met them in Panama City.

The group went out to the farm where the owning family supposedly supported forty-seven missionaries.

The Caballero family, led by Elias and Lorenzo, met the group on the porch. With Steve Nolen interpreting, conversations began. Greg grew impatient and started asking questions. Most importantly for the business, "Are you going to let us buy coffee or not?"

Elias communicated that Greg should wait. They wanted to be friends first.

Greg sulked at first, but over the next few days as they visited different places, Brian and Greg started to hear the story of the Caballero family.

A Legacy of Faith

The Caballero farm in Panama is run by ten brothers and sisters who support missions and church planting and other relief around the world with the profits from the coffee.

But it almost didn't happen.

Their father owned the farm first, and the children witnessed how the father would give to pastors and missionaries and anyone else who had need. He would give little bits of money here and there over the years. Some of the recipients they saw. Many they didn't.

Once their father went into a restaurant with around ten dollars to buy food for the family. He came out with nothing. The story he told was of a hungry family, a woman and her children. This family had nothing. The father used the money to buy them what he could. "We have plenty," he said. That family had nothing. The Caballero family had rice and beans again.

The father would inconvenience the family with his generosity. He brought in a blind boy, who had been abandoned, to live with them. Ten children became eleven, with another mouth to feed.

They took string and used it to line paths around the house and property—from the front door to the bathroom, to the kitchen, outside to the chicken houses—so the blind boy could find his way around the house and yard. Lorenzo spoke of having to duck to get under the string all over the house. He would later connect the lesson with one of humility and service to God, but as a young man, he resented it.

Elias remembers wearing jeans with holes in them.

Their father had been generous, but the Caballero family saw their lack, how finances had been kept from them, that his giving heart was to their detriment. They associated the coffee farm with this resentment.

When their father died, the ten children agreed. They would sell the farm and split the money between them. They didn't want to continue the family business.

At their father's funeral, a crowd of people appeared, far more than they expected.

For hours they heard stories with the same pattern. A woman would come up and describe a crisis in the family. "Then your father ..." A pastor spoke of a struggling church and said, "Then your father ..."

The stories seemed endless. One after another. Over and over. Life after life impacted by their father's generosity. Lives changed and saved.

Then the children understood. They couldn't sell the farm. They had to keep it and continue their father's legacy.

For Brian and Greg, the stories of the Caballero patriarch reminded them of their friend Joe Wingo at Angel Food Ministries, a man who had been generous to so many people. Those they both had helped were ready and willing to speak of their generosity.

After the funeral, God told the family to gather their money, all the cash they had. They had $2,001.00 in the year 2001. But what would they do with it? Lorenzo, Elias, and their siblings fasted and prayed while walking around the farm.

While on his knees in the field praying, God told Lorenzo to stand up and tell his family to put the money in tomato seeds and fertilizer.

Lorenzo did so.

This was a strange instruction for a family of coffee farmers. They prayed together and got confirmation. Yes, God was telling them to buy tomato seeds and fertilizer.

They didn't know anything about tomatoes. They asked God what to do with the seeds.

Plant them in between the coffee trees, God told them.

They obeyed, buying the seeds and planting the tomatoes.

The next season, there was a tomato blight in Panama. Every tomato farm in Panama helplessly watched as their crop turned yellow and brown, withering and dying.

Every crop but one farm's, that is.

The Caballero farm in the mountains was the only one that didn't suffer the blight. They were the only ones with tomatoes in the country. The price of tomatoes skyrocketed. The normal price was five cents a pound. That season, the Caballeros sold for ninety cents a pound.

As an added benefit to figuring out how to plant and fertilize tomatoes with coffee, the Caballeros started harvesting their coffee crop every two years instead of the standard three.

365 Ministry

Greg continued to ask questions. What did it mean for them to support forty-seven missionaries?

Lorenzo explained that in the context of the political and religious history of their culture, many Latino missionaries would come simply looking for a handout. The Caballeros would commit to 75 percent of the salary, but the missionaries had to earn the other 25 percent to give them ownership and responsibility in the ministry.

After the growing success with the coffee, the Caballeros asked what God wanted them to do with all this.

They first prayed and fasted again while walking around the farm. Late one Sunday night, they walked and came to a goat trail. They followed the goat trail and came to a shack. A light shone within the shack, and a young man knelt in front of the little building. He was praying.

God told the Caballeros to give the man five dollars.

They approached the young man and gently interrupted him. "God told us to give you five dollars"

The man saw the money and began to weep.

The Caballeros asked why he was weeping.

He told them he was the pastor of the church behind him. He meant the shack. His wife had given birth, but they didn't have anything for the baby. They needed to buy formula to feed the child. The young pastor told God he wasn't going home without money to buy formula. The church collection had been $0.43. Formula cost $5.43.

That experience birthed a vision for the Caballeros that they would support 365 missionaries and bush pastors—one for every day of the year, and from that idea came the El Semprador 365 Ministry. In English, *el semprador* means "the sower.".

And they began to work toward that goal. Because of the political conflicts and a negative perception of those from the United States, missionaries from Central America can get into countries that Americans never could. For many of the countries hostile to the gospel, these missionaries from Latin American countries are bringing relief and the gospel through the Caballero family.

Taking Inventory

Brian and Greg went with the Caballeros to meet others in Panama.

Highlands Coffee Roasters in Boquete was run by Jose David and his father. Brian and Greg drank some of the best coffee they'd ever tasted and heard more stories.

Jose David was a Christian, and one night he couldn't sleep. God kept telling him to count the beans. Jose David woke up his cousin Javier Pitti, who worked with him, and told him they had to have a full inventory of all the bean they possessed from their farm.

Javier balked. That would take a long time!

Jose David knew it would take a massive effort, but he couldn't get away from God's instruction. He had to say yes. They had to do a complete inventory—where the coffee came from, the tasting profiles, and exactly how much they had. All of it was recorded and written down.

Javier told Jose David about this pile of trash bean they had. Jose David directed him to put the trash bean to the side. They would sell it cheap to Folgers or someone similar.

The day after they finished the inventory, a car drove up with a man who asked for their inventory.

Which they now had.

The man asked for a bean with a specific type of flavor profile. He looked through the log and found what he wanted: the bean they set aside to sell for nothing, cents a pound if they were lucky, the trash bean. That was what he wanted. Could he get some?

Of course.

The man asked how much David and Javier wanted for the bean.

They asked him how much he would pay.

He responded, sixty dollars a pound.

The Highlands Roasters agreed to that price.

The man asked how much of the bean they had.

They asked him how much he wanted.

He said he needed one hundred pounds, and they sold it to him for sixty dollars a pound. The man put the one hundred pounds of coffee in backpacks, loaded them into his car, and left.

That coffee eventually made it to New York at a formal cupping and won first place. This came to be known as Geisha coffee and transformed the financial situation of Highland Coffee Company.

The story further confirmed the heart of the Phoenix Roasters ministry to Brian and Greg. Bean that would be considered trash was highly valued, transformed from nothing to the top-specialty coffee in the land. Everything changed when someone said yes to God.

Why Do I Know What I Know?

Javier Pitti prepared the coffee cupping while Brian and Greg were at Highland Coffee Roasters. Javier was a well-known roaster, consistently ranked in the top five of Latino roasters. He had mentored the people who roasted coffee for the emperor of Japan. Japan sent their Imperial tea roasters to learn coffee roasting from Javier.

This was a humble and modest man who built coffee roasters in his backyard with sheet metal and used car parts.

During the cupping, Javier heard Brian explain the vision and purpose of Phoenix Community and Phoenix Roasters.

That's what friends do. They share stories.

The stories were all told through an interpreter, and when Brian finished describing the mission of Phoenix Community and Phoenix Roasters, Javier started crying.

Javier had been praying and asking God why he knew what he knew about coffee. While Brian shared, he knew why. It became clear.

"When you were sharing, God spoke to me," Javier said. "I want to train you to be the best roasters of Panamanian coffee bean in the United States."

Javier normally charged $500 or more an hour to teach someone how to roast coffee. He offered to teach Phoenix Roasters for free.

A close family and partnership developed and deepened between the Caballeros and Phoenix Roasters.

Did Phoenix Roasters buy the coffee? Yes. But it was about more than business and money. As Phoenix Roasters learned with the Mejia family while asking for the roaster, these farmers and their families desired relationship.

Coffee is the second most-traded commodity in the world, behind oil. Coffee is traded six or seven times before it gets from the farm to the coffee shop or bag on a shelf in the store. Even within fair-trade coffee, the farmers get far less. In a world where Western businessmen buy internationally for as cheap as they can for the biggest profit, it became even more important that Phoenix Roasters treats these amazing business people and farmers with dignity and respect.

The relationship that developed was one of equity and value where Phoenix Roasters bought the coffee for an excellent price, directly, cutting out the six or seven middlemen. The greater price for coffee gave the Caballeros margin to pay their employees dignified and sustainable wages and support missionaries.

The Caballeros aren't only business partners. They are family. They've come to visit Phoenix Roasters in Atlanta, working at conferences. When groups from Phoenix Roasters take trips down to Panama, they stay in the Caballero home on the farm. Living together. Praying together. Singing together. Telling stories.

The principles built upon one another. From the initial idea of a marketplace church to Young Life coffee directly supporting missions to Perry Walker igniting the mindset of direct trade with indigenous mission-minded farmers, God led through one yes after another.

Now it was time to take Javier up on his offer to become the best coffee roasters in America.

Exploration

This is the age of authenticity. People want to know that we care, that we can relate to the hard times they are going through. The Phoenix Community pastors have been wounded and weary too, which gives us an understanding and camaraderie with those broken and hurting. We don't come to people as professional Christians. We bring our own stories of hardship, struggle, and overcoming when ministering to the broken.

When God made a plan to save the whole world, He came down and lived among us. He suffered the same injustices and oppression of His people. He "faced all the same testings we do, yet he did not sin" (Hebrews 4:15). Jesus became one of us to meet us there and transform us.

Paul also spoke of being "all things to all people," whether Jew or Gentile, whatever the culture and context, to save some. He was willing to meet people where they were to invite them into eternal life (1 Corinthians 9:22–23 NIV).

In stage four of the Favor Cycle, how well we endure the storms of life determines our influence in the lives of others.

People relate to our stories and listen to those with similar experience. One person who has overcome something difficult or tragic—addiction, abuse, unemployment, rejection, grief, etc.—brings hope to others that transformation is possible. This is why the three-word story from earlier is central to the Phoenix Community. Stories of transformation lead to more people rising from the ashes of life.

Those who have been broken and healed by the love of the Father can reach out to others with more compassion and understanding. That is a more loving and universal place to start or deepen relationships than by how we are different or disagree.

We call this principle "like-brokennness." Like-brokenness attracts; different-mindedness repels.

What are some ways you could use the storms of your life to connect with others? How have your own wounds and griefs made you more compassionate to those going through difficult times? Are you, your family, and your church attractive to those who are broken?

Spend time in prayer asking God whom you could reach out to and share your story of brokenness and healing with. Write those names down with ideas of how you will reach out to them.

_____

_____

_____

_____

_____

_____

_____

_____

_____

_____

_____

_____

_____

_____

CHAPTER 10
Roasting and Guatemala

S ometimes we get more than we ask for.

Tommy Holland, Brian's father, was heavily involved in his church and went on mission trips over the years. While in Guatemala City, Guatemala, in February 2012, Tommy called to check in with the family. He spoke with Brian.

Brian and the Phoenix Community pastors were still searching for a coffee source, before even meeting with Perry Walker at the conference. Talking with his father, Brian said, "While you're there, look for some good coffee guys."

He was half joking.

Tommy Holland was a successful lawyer in Atlanta and believed in his son's vision. He did look for some good coffee guys.

A man on the trip with Tommy was familiar with Guatemala and spoke fluent Spanish, and in the many relationships began that week, they met someone at Lake Atitlán who heard of this family nearby that grew specialty-grade coffee in the volcanic soil. And they were Christians who supported pastors. Tommy wanted to meet with this family, the Navichocs.

Irving Navichoc didn't want to take the meeting. He had met with a lot of people who made promises, and he never heard from them again. But in an effort to be nice and polite, he took the meeting with Tommy.

Months later, Tommy and Brian returned with a pastor friend from another church looking for ministry and business-mission opportunities, and that had never happened before. Many people had met the Navichocs with promises to return and do ministry in connection with the coffee, but no one ever came back.

Tommy did.

Irving was connected with a pastor in a rural village, Pastor Rafael, who had been going into the village of San Juan Moca to do church gatherings on Sundays and serve the people. San Juan Moca was one of the poorest and most violent areas in Guatemala and close to Irving's heart.

Phoenix Roasters recognized an opportunity to get involved and bring relief even before importing coffee.

With one missional coffee source locked in and another on the way, Phoenix Roasters transitioned into the New Year with things looking up.

Grind It Out

While serving as the youth pastor in his former church prior to starting Phoenix Community, Brian connected with Jeff Foxworthy, whose daughter was on the basketball team Brian coached. Brian and Ginney's daughter Emily and Jeff's daughter were on the team together.

After that season, Brian and Jeff rarely saw each other, but at a chance meeting at a high school volleyball game, Jeff recognized Ginney. Jeff and Ginney were both there to cheer on their nieces, who played for the same team.

Jeff asked Ginney for Brian's phone number and invited him to come down to the Atlanta Mission to help with a Bible study he had started early on Tuesday mornings for men who were emerging out of homelessness.

The Atlanta Mission is one of the premier homeless programs in the South with both a homeless shelter that provides meals for men and women living on the street and a well-developed, faith-based program that teaches, houses, and counsels men to overcome addiction and move forward in transformative ways.

Jeff believed in the work of the Atlanta Mission and started a Bible study for the men in the program. Brian agreed to help and take one of the classes. Some leaders brought donuts; Jeff stopped by Chick-fil-A to get one hundred biscuits to share with the men in the program. Brian noticed that the coffee brought in wasn't top quality, so he took over that part of the breakfast on Tuesdays, bringing excellent, high-quality coffee.

This is where Phoenix Roasters developed the term Wedding Feast Coffee. Jesus always brings the best to anyone who would receive it, and Phoenix Roasters felt the same.

Brian, Greg, and Jeff (Bagwell) invited Jeff (Foxworthy) in for a meeting in February 2013 to explore ways that he could help the small but growing business. There was coffee to pay for. Salaries to pay for. Churches to plant.

Jeff Foxworthy kindly agreed to be on the coffee board for Phoenix Roasters and use his influence in any way he could, but he never reached for his checkbook, which would have been welcome to a small coffee company still struggling to survive.

Instead he said, "I think God's telling me that you should grind it out. It makes for a better story."

Grind it out.

Forget All That

Wes Patterson loved working with his hands, so he enjoyed being taught what little Brian knew of roasting and continuing to help the coffee company in that capacity.

For Brian, head pastor of Phoenix Community and head of Phoenix Roasters, the actual task of roasting took more and more time away from his other responsibilities. It was a natural choice to send Wes down to be taught how to be the best roaster in the US.

For Wes, movies like *End of the Spear* inspired his idea of missions. Often what God asks people to do for the gospel seems the opposite of good sense or sound strategy.

Wes and Becky Patterson took a trip down to Panama. They spent time with the Caballeros, saw the farm, and then took a trip out to Boquete to be trained by Javier Pitti.

Javier had an older double barrel two-pound Probat roaster in Panama that he had to adjust with a computer that helped to blow air into the flame. At the high altitude, the airflow was a problem. Javier is both an artist and an engineer at heart. The master roaster had all the gadgets to test density and humidity.

What Wes knew was a timed system—after a few minutes, turn the heat up, modify airflow—each task completed at certain points in a timed process.

On the first day in Boquete, Javier asked him, "Tell me what you know."

Wes explained his method with a stopwatch.

Javier said, "No! Forget all that."

Over the next few days, Javier taught Wes roasting intricacies on that small cupping roaster, because if Wes could learn on that, he could roast on anything. After hours of learning at the feet of the master on the smaller Probat roaster, Javier then brought Wes back to his house to introduce him to the roasting machine Javier had built from scrap and junk parts. Javier named his home roaster Joppy.

Communication was difficult with Wes's minimal Spanish and Javier's minimal English, but the two men became friends during the experience.

Instead of a timed approach, Javier taught what was happening to the bean and why. What would temperature do? What would more airflow do? Javier taught what to do at different cracks to make the bean respond in ways that would retain the flavor of the bean.

The bitterness most associate with coffee is due to poor brewing methods and burning the bean during the roast. With cheap and low-quality bean, maintaining the flavor isn't the goal. When the bean is specialty, high-quality Arabica, preserving the flavor is paramount, and that takes skilled roasting.

A master.

Great roasting can't improve a bad bean. But awful roasting can ruin a great bean. The Caballero Panamanian was great bean.

Javier roasted a few times, showing Wes everything he did. Then he told Wes, "Okay, now you roast."

Wes practiced with a six-ounce roast, doing his best to replicate the master with the Panamanian bean.

Later the whole team came in to do a coffee cupping of Javier's roast. There was coffee from different regions and even the Geisha coffee. Becky tried many of the coffees, but kept coming back to the Geisha.

Javier didn't reveal which one was Wes Patterson's, and at the end of the cupping experience, he pointed to one of the roasts and asked everyone what they thought.

Everyone agreed. It wasn't as good.

Javier laughed. That one was roasted by Wes!

Wes spent two days with Javier in Panama on that first trip, which was an amazing opportunity. He returned to America and the Probat at the warehouse in Atlanta, trying to figure out the best way to mimic and put into practice Javier's methods.

One of Wes's lesser-known talents, although very familiar to his family and friends, is his ability to mimic voices. Those close to him get to hear different singers or maybe Will Ferrell's Harry Caray impersonation on a regular basis. He enjoys mimicking, and the time with Javier and roasting was no different.

Wes and Javier became friends on Facebook, and with the great tool of social media, Wes was able to ask questions and get more instruction.

In 2014 Wes went back for two more days with Javier, learning from the master. Another year, the Caballeros came to Atlanta and further assisted Wes as he worked with the Probat to find the best ways to roast the Panamanian bean.

The original temperature gauge on the Probat in Atlanta was decades of degrees off and unreliable, causing Wes to roast more and more by sound of crack and feel than a reliable temperature. When Phoenix Roasters was able to finally buy the Probat L12 from the Mejia family, Wes drilled into the center with a probe connected to a new digital gauge in it to get more accurate temperatures to combine the sound and feel of roasting.

Serving Coffee to Thousands of People

During this time Phoenix Roasters also began serving coffee at conferences.

The initial goal and vision for Phoenix Roasters was to sell to different churches to use on Sunday morning and for fundraising. The important contacts were churches, therefore, and serving excellent coffee and telling the story of the company at conferences became a focus. Because of their former work at large Baptist churches, the pastors began to look into different possibilities.

The first conference for Phoenix Roasters was one for youth leaders and volunteers called Conclave, which met annually in Chattanooga, Tennessee. The pastors made their way up to the conference in trucks and trailers full of pieced-together equipment and whatever they could scrounge together—brewers, coffee cambros, cups, and more. Brian, Greg, and Jeff laugh at the comparison to the Clampetts from *Beverly Hillbillies*, which comes up often.

They stayed in a house together on Lookout Mountain. They may not have been as prepared as they needed to be, but they worked hard and served the attendees with pride and love, telling their story and passing out cards and networking as much as they could.

The next conference was Send in Woodstock, Georgia, and then another in Dallas. Phoenix Roasters learned how to be more efficient and effective as a company at these events.

Working conferences also allowed Phoenix Roasters to see the church from a kingdom-eye view. So often in the "church world," the "bigger, better" world that the pastors extricated themselves from, competition is the ugly underbelly of many ministries.

In the South particularly, a Methodist church sits next to a Baptist or a charismatic fellowship, often several along the same street. As Brian experienced before leaving his "big church," many of these fellowships competed for the smaller percentage of people already going to church instead of evangelizing the unchurched in the community.

Brian and Greg already had experience meeting and supporting other student pastors in years past. The idea of seeing all churches through a kingdom lens wasn't difficult for the Phoenix Community crew trying to do church in a different way.

Perhaps the church next door wasn't a competitor but a friend. Perhaps churches that believed in Jesus were all on the same team.

The marginalized, hurting, and addicted cared less for the denominational affiliation than they did how they were treated and the healing offered. Phoenix offered a way for all churches and believers to be on the same team by simply doing something they already did every Sunday at almost every church in America—drink coffee.

But instead of drinking horrible coffee that contributed to the slave wages seen on farms overseas, Phoenix Roasters sold coffee that gave dignified prices for the coffee directly to mission-minded farmers who in turn paid sustainable wages to their workers. The coffee supported missions and church planting in America and all over the world.

And Phoenix Roasters coffee tasted more and more amazing as they became better at roasting quality bean.

In this way, pastors could connect with other pastors over what was important—the kingdom, evangelism, missions—with a simple but amazing drink on Sunday mornings. They could all be on the same team.

An inspiring principle, to be sure. However, even with miraculous God stories and an amazing cup of coffee, change in the church world can be difficult. A few churches signed on and the company grew, but it wasn't the exponential uptick Phoenix Roasters hoped for.

They were, as Jeff Foxworthy said, grinding it out.

What some of these pastors needed was to see for themselves the families transformed by the coffee. A story is important, but a shared experience is even better. Now that Phoenix had friends in Panama and Guatemala, they decided to start taking mission trips to these places to show that these were more than stories. People experienced hope and transformation in the poorest of places.

Brian, Greg, Jeff, and Wes wanted to share their lives with other Christians and pastors on mission. Making friends.

God led Phoenix Community to do church differently. Then He orchestrated them to do coffee business differently.

Now the Father would open their eyes in ways to do missions differently.

As you can guess, they said yes.

Exploration

Stage five of the Favor Cycle brings us back to the beginning to stage one. The amount of influence we have in other people's lives is the opportunity to speak truth and grace into their story.

God gives more favor to those who have been good stewards of it. What does it mean to be good stewards of His favor?

The influence we have in the lives of others isn't to point to ourselves or for our own worldly wealth or success. Our influence in the lives of others is for the glory of God, to make Him famous because it is all about Him (Romans 11:36).

We reveal who God is.

He is good. All good things come from Him. His grace is unmerited. His favor is unlimited.

Our good is wrapped up in His glory. The angels declared the night of Jesus' birth: "Glory to God in highest heaven, and peace on earth to those with whom God is pleased" (Luke 2:14). Glorifying God brings peace and goodwill to people, an increase of favor.

Pray for God to center your heart on the purpose of His glory and making Him famous. Thinking of His character and His actions, write down five things (at least!) you want to the world to know about God.

_____

_____

_____

_____

_____

_____

_____

CHAPTER 11
Transformissional

What does it mean to help a person? A community? Is it possible the church and missions have done it wrong?

Two books greatly influenced the way Phoenix Community and Phoenix Roasters does relief and missions: *Toxic Charity* by Robert Lupton and *When Helping Hurts* by Steve Corbett and Brian Fikkert. And as Phoenix Community drew closer to taking people on mission trips to places like Panama and Guatemala, a member of Phoenix Community in Duluth put the pastors in touch with the author of *Toxic Charity*, Robert "Bob" Lupton.

Bob's influence led Phoenix Community to adopt the idea of the "dignity of exchange," both in the US and overseas, an idea that no one has nothing. Instead of seeing and treating people as less because they may happen to have less, missions and relief must treat people with the dignity that they come to the relationship with skills, talents, and resources.

In the meeting, Bob described a common occurrence over Christmas, how churches would roll into a high-poverty area, like an apartment complex. The church passes out toys for the kids, the kids would be happy, and their mothers would come with them. But the fathers were always absent.

Why? For the fathers, being unable to provide for their children over Christmas engendered feelings of failure, and the church coming in to give presents to the family reminded them of that failure, compounding those negative feelings.

Brian cringed. Phoenix had done that exact thing the Christmas before.

A more successful opportunity would be to set up a system that employed the men for the day and gave them money for gifts, perhaps making the donated toys available at discounted prices. This would empower the men, making them feel better about themselves and proud of providing for their family.

This is the dignity of exchange.

Another important principle was that missions should go in under a local authority in the country where they are operating. When churches or ministries come in for a week as "American saviors" and hand out money and candy and gifts, they set themselves up as the source of relief, undercutting the authority of the local and indigenous leadership. But then the American missionaries leave. The local leadership remains to deal with the fallout of an influx of material goods and entertainment instead of lasting change.

Both *Toxic Charity* and *When Helping Hurts* suggest a more dignified approach, and Phoenix Roasters was encouraged to find a local authority that could help provide relief, employment, and ministry in Guatemala.

Bob looked at the pastors. "I hope you guys aren't thinking you're taking Jesus there."

After an awkward moment, the pastors responded, "Of course we are." That's what missions is all about. Right? We'll take Jesus there.

"I want to suggest, for your prayerful consideration," Bob said, "that Jesus has been there a long time."

Phoenix Community began taking mission trips with these ideas as a foundation. To treat people like they have something rather than lacking. Not only because it was empowering. But because it was true.

San Juan Moca

The first mission trip to Guatemala was in 2013. Brian took his daughter Emily and three people from a partner church. Brian was the first white man the village had ever seen.

They built a house in San Juan Moca while on the trip, all while under the authority of Pastor Rafael Puac Trejo. The people from America were told not to bring candy or any gifts. All work and relief would be done through Pastor Rafael and the local church.

San Juan Moca had been identified by the coffee farmers, the Navichocs, as the poorest village in the area. While Pastor Rafael and Maria lived one hundred kilometers away, they were from the same indigenous tribe as the village. In 2005, the mountain village had been cut off from civilization by Hurricane Stan. All roads in and out were destroyed and never rebuilt, throwing the village and people further into poverty and creating the perfect environment for gangs to terrorize the village.

Pastor Rafael and his wife Maria weren't well received when they arrived to begin ministry. The town leaders didn't like how the pastors counseled women not to have so many children. For the women, their perception of their value was primarily in bearing children. The women dealt with transient working men who would stay for a while, have a couple kids, and then leave for other employment opportunities.

The gangs placed everyone in danger, as well, which made Maria feel unsafe, and she thought they should leave. Rafael needed to protect his family.

The gang activity became so prevalent that the community unified together in the middle of the night, made a stand, and violently removed the gang leaders from the area.

Rafael and Maria kept coming back. They lived near Lake Atitlán but would travel into the village for Sunday services.

The first house Phoenix Community built was for an older woman in the village. She has passed now, but her son lives there today, where he is building his family and serves as a deacon in Pastor Rafael's church.

Phoenix Community's continued and faithful investment in the village opened the door for other churches and ministries to work in San Juan Moca. Brian was not only the first white man they saw in the village, but he returned a few times that year and then again the next year.

Just like Phoenix showed with Irving Navichoc, they came back. Believing in the importance of relationships and that true transformation is a long process, Phoenix Community still works to improve the village and their resources.

Because they came in under Rafael's authority, the years of work by Phoenix Community and other groups in the village also brought credibility to the pastor and the church. After years of these groups bringing more value to the community, the village council walked into the church on a Sunday morning during worship, marched up the stairs, and stopped the service.

They had an announcement to make to the village. They could no longer ignore Pastor Rafael's contribution to the community. The council wanted to celebrate the pastor and asked him to join the town council, an amazing statement of his impact.

See the Transformation

Transformation takes time, and Phoenix Community has been taking groups down to Guatemala since 2013.

Today San Juan Moca has better housing and sanitation. Simple things like bathrooms were built and added to houses in the village. Trash was once piled everywhere. Now the church and the community work together to pick up trash and place it in a dump truck.

Whenever work is done in the village to build a home, bathroom, or villa for the teachers, local construction crews are hired, making several times their normal wage, which helps their families and the community.

A few trips have included basic medical care. A Guatemalan doctor came to the village with one group and gave advice and simple medicines. That same trip, the group bought several pairs of eyeglasses with different prescriptions. People from the village lined up to try on glasses if they needed them. One older woman wept at seeing clearly for the first time in years.

Education has been a major focus of the mission work. Phoenix Community has given resources for the village school and extra money for teachers. Steve Fulton, one of Phoenix Roasters's coffee partners, had already been involved with missions in Guatemala.

Steve is known as Papa Grande and visited San Juan Moca with Phoenix Community one summer. Papa Grande and his home church have helped to improve the school and give teachers Bibles with their names engraved on them as well. Many teachers wept at receiving their first Bible.

The village school only goes up through middle school. The only way for a student to continue their education after the village school costs more money and hours of travel time. Phoenix Community began giving partial scholarships to students, making them work for the rest as a part of the "dignity of exchange."

This past year, the first two participants in that scholarship program graduated from high school. Not only does Phoenix Community celebrate that success, but the example of excellence, hope, and opportunity for the rural village is immense.

Phoenix Community has begun work on a program where kids are fed and tutored after school to better prepare them for higher education. The first two people they want to hire for the program are the first two students that graduated from high school.

When Phoenix Community comes to the village, no one begs the Americans for money. The people and children of the village see the local church and their own pastor as the authority. That's where they'll find relief. This allows people from America to build relationships, especially those that come year after year.

In the beginning, Pastor Rafael was concerned with his church in the village. All his attention was focused there and that desperate situation. Over time and through the change in San Juan Moca, he has planted two churches in other parts of Guatemala and was elevated to a staff position at his sending church.

Transformissional

The ultimate success for Phoenix Roasters is the relationships that happen. The mountains and volcanic lakes inspire with their views, and it might be good for business to bring people on mission. But it is about the people—both those overseas and those who go on the trip.

Greg Sweatt came up with the term for the trips. They are transformissional—people are transformed as they go on mission. Many come back "ruined" for a normal American life. Returning to a land of abundance after seeing poverty and need opens minds and hearts to consumer choices and the impact they have on a daily basis. Those on the trips are told not to give money directly. Relationships are the most important value. Learn a child's name. Communicate with him or her the best you can.

Everyone has their own experience. People with little or no faith come on a trip, and yet their lives are still changed to see the real impact that relief and relationship can have in the world. They become more generous. They view people with dignity.

No matter the beginning point, people grow as disciples of Christ.

While on the trips, Phoenix Community has seen people commit their hearts to God for the first time or a veteran minister receive a new vision for reaching out and bringing relief in his or her community in the US.

One young man who went on a trip with Phoenix Community to Guatemala had lost both of his parents within one year of each other while he was in high school. He was a close friend of someone at Phoenix Community in Duluth and attended the high school where Brian was the chaplain for the football team. Brian got involved and provided what help the church could during that difficult time.

Years later the young man moved back to Duluth and started attending Phoenix Community in Duluth. He saved up money and went on the trip to Guatemala. Upon his return, he wrote about his change in perspective, looking forward to the positives of what God was going to do in his life instead of the pain of the past: "I used to think, 'Why me?' Now I think, 'What's next?'"

Phoenix Community began doing missions in Guatemala before the coffee company officially purchased coffee from the Navichocs. The company got the first shipment of specialty coffee from Irving and the family in 2014.

Stories of transformation in other countries from missional coffee inspire people, but nothing takes the place of personal experience. Bringing people on mission to Guatemala and the coffee fields has the added benefit of creating hyperfans, people who have seen firsthand the amazing economic and social change from dignified trade, relief, and relationship. These hyperfans tell friends and colleagues and try to get others to buy the coffee. They not only tell the story of the coffee; they have their own.

But Guatemala wasn't the only place Phoenix Community took trips. They brought friends to their family with the Caballeros in Panama. With all of these connections, Phoenix Community began to experience the exponential growth of mission and relief.

Exploration

Many who go on mission trips return and talk about how they feel they got more out of it than they gave.

This is the way of the kingdom. God is a giver—for God so loved that He gave His Son (John 3:16)—and when we participate in giving and generosity, we experience more intimacy and joy walking in his character.

Phoenix Community and Phoenix Roasters have learned that dignifying people includes expecting that they have something to give too and that we have something to receive from them. God desires for us to love one another (John 13:34), and we expect that ministry will not happen only one way. Paul's use of the physical body as an example of how the church works is important (1 Corinthians 12). No part of our body exists for itself but gives life to other parts and receives as well.

As Bob Lupton told us, we should realize God has already been working in the places we go.

Phoenix Community calls our trips *transformissional* for this reason. We build into our trips the expectation that God is out to transform us and the people we minister to as we move forward on mission.

Pray for more humility and revelation of how to receive from others no matter who or where they are because of the great value they hold in God's eyes.

Write down an example of a time you ministered Christ to others and felt enormously blessed by God in the moment.

CHAPTER 12
The Global Cycle of Relief

Brian had a toy he loved as a kid—a Hot Wheels track that went in a figure eight. At the middle intersection in that figure, there was an accelerator that shot the cars forward to go around the track one more time.

The Hot Wheels track became a model for what Phoenix Roasters began to experience. On one side sat the farmers, the workers, the children, and the relief efforts of medication, education, and vocation. On the other side sat Phoenix Roasters the coffee company and the Phoenix Community of Atlanta. The global intersection connected those in the US with those around the world.

Who were the accelerators in the middle? That intersection represented those who bought Phoenix Roasters coffee—individuals, churches, nonprofits, businesses, and more. We call this model the Global Cycle of Relief. When explaining this model to his wife, Ginney, she observed that if you turned the eight on its side it becomes the infinity symbol.

Infinity. The eternal kingdom of God. The things that last forever are the things that matter.

Staying with Family

In 2013 Phoenix Community took the first trip to Panama, where we joined in the work—and stayed in the family home—of the Caballeros, who were already bringing relief in their community.

In the town near the coffee farm, the hospital provided meals to the poorer children who had to stay on a long-term basis and for the mothers who visited them. The hospital didn't provide these meals on Saturdays or Sundays. The Caballeros would bring food for the families on Saturdays and Sundays and pray with them. Groups from the US would go with them for that ministry.

The common housing for workers on the field was a shack, normal for most of Central America. The Caballeros wanted to improve the workers' housing, so Phoenix Roasters began bringing mission groups from America to live on the farm and build housing with running water and electricity. After five years of trips and work, the long process of providing housing was finished. Now the workers have bathrooms and showers.

The Caballeros are also passionate about providing respite housing for pastors. Planting churches and pastoring in rural areas in Central America is a difficult job, and the family started building a place for pastors to come and take some time to rest. This facility will also be open to missionaries coming home from the field for a vacation or break from their mission.

The Caballeros have developed another program to help employ people and dignify them with work. The Caballeros own more land on the mountain that could be cleared and planted for food or coffee. Instead they decided to offer the land for free to people if they would be responsible to clear the land and plant crops. A dozen or more have accepted this amazing offer, learning how to plant and feeding their families.

God has even provided a man with the resources to put money toward the project, to help these families clear the land.

Connecting Our Stories

God shows up when we live life together, when we express the truth that we are connected beyond the physical. Taking groups from America to a house on a farm in Panama produces God moments.

One young man from a Baptist church went with Greg Sweatt on a trip to Panama and stayed with the Caballero family. The group and the farmers shared stories and offered prayers together as a family one in Christ, and the young man shared his own story.

He had started attending an evangelical church, coming to Christ and getting heavily involved. His mother was Catholic and didn't like or understand her son's religious experience. She resisted his involvement in the church and was unwilling to discuss the matter.

He asked his grandmother to help him communicate with her daughter, his mother. The grandmother said, "Just tell her you found your song."

When the young man and his sister were younger, their grandmother would sing a song over them, as she had done the mother before. The song? "How Great Thou Art." When the young man explained this to his mother, she began to understand what his relationship with Jesus and his new church meant to him. Their relationship improved.

With Phoenix Community, it is important to learn how to tell your story in three words, and they help people choose those words while on a mission trip. This young man had *song* as one of his words as a result of his grandmother's advice.

Elias Caballero had been quiet and distant all week. Making excuses about money and hardship, he had not been there with the group Greg brought the week before. Greg paid Elias Jr. (Elias's son) to be the interpreter for the first trip, which had also been an amazing, Spirit-filled time. After that week, Elias Jr. used the money he made translating and gave it to his father to come be on the trip.

While the young man told his story at the family home, Greg looked over and saw that Elias Sr. wept. Lorenzo also had his head down, and a heaviness filled the room.

Once the young man finished his story, Greg spoke to the Caballeros. "You know that song?"

Lorenzo said, "Yes. That was our father's song."

"Can you sing it with us?" Greg asked.

As the group started singing, Elias Sr. turned around, lifted his hands in the air, and sang "How Great Thou Art" in Spanish. The rest of the family raised their voices in Spanish. The Americans sang the song in English. The presence of God filled the room.

The song ended, and there was a prayer. Greg wondered what had happened with the family. Why were Elias and the family so upset?

Greg learned that Elias Sr. had been battling depression, money issues, and family conflict. The family hadn't been together in worship like that for a long time.

Pulling Elias Sr. and Elias Jr. aside, Greg told Elias Jr. to translate what he said. "Isn't it great to have a son that loves you so much he would pay to have you with him?"

That moment was a turning point in reconciliation between members of the family and better relationships.

Empowering with a Co-op

Phoenix Roasters met Greg Hines through First Baptist Atlanta, Charles Stanley's church. Greg worked in missions and had begun setting up co-ops in 2012. By 2013, Greg and his wife Jean were living down in Honduras full-time, empowering the local farmers and businesspeople and planting churches.

While in Honduras, Greg and Jean started Cocatecal, a co-op of rural coffee growers in the community of Cruz Alta. Thirty-five families comprise the co-op, some of them single mothers. The co-op pools the resources of its members to produce large quantities and compete in the market while allowing rural farms to maintain ownership and control of their family-owned land. A total of 165 people receive benefits due to the membership with Cocatecal.

The co-op owns its own de-pulping and washing stations complete with large drying patios for the bean, oven dryers, and warehousing. All of it is located near the farms. These resources have allowed the farmers to produce a higher-quality bean, which then results in being able to charge higher prices.

The farmers have access to low-cost financing, technical assistance, and quality control through the co-op.

Too often the natural resources of places like Central America are destroyed or ruined for the sake of profit. Creating environmentally friendly businesses and farms is important to Cocatecal, so a part of the technical training the farmers receive teaches them to farm in ways that preserve the beautiful environment, including better handling the wastewater produced during the washing process and participating in tree-planting initiatives that restore mountain forests and the environment.

The low-cost financing surely helps, but the Hines and the co-op have goals of long-term self-sustainability of the farmers and their families independent of banks or other institutions. Improving the quality of coffee and fetching higher than fair-trade prices for the coffee are the pathways to seeing more and more families become independent and sustainable.

Two years ago a farmer had an exceptional harvest and reported he was able to upgrade his own de-pulping station and provide some luxuries for his family that included a new, bigger, and more comfortable mattress for him and his wife.

Cocatecal has impact beyond coffee. In partnership with another organization the co-op donates one cent per pound to Amigos del Café, a nonprofit relief organization. Amigos del Café funds community development projects and educational resources for kids in coffee-growing areas.

These projects include health education, installing concreted floors in homes, and stuffing backpacks with school supplies for the children to start the new school year.

Greg and Jean Hines have also helped plant churches in the area.

Staying in contact over the years with such a similar heart for ministry, Greg Sweatt and Wes Patterson traveled to Honduras in September 2015. They stayed with Greg and Jean at their home in Honduras and met with the co-op members and pastors ready to plant churches.

After working with the co-op to improve the quality of the coffee through better farming methods, Phoenix Roasters began importing Honduran coffee from the co-op—a third missional coffee source in addition to Panamanian and Guatemalan.

Redemptive Trade

It is often difficult to discuss the model of trade that Phoenix Roasters uses because it is not simply business oriented. It's not only ministry focused. It is both, and it also encompasses a relational component that goes beyond even what most within Fair Trade or missional coffee achieve.

Wes Patterson and I attended a conference dealing with Christians using coffee as an avenue to bring missions to the world. The conference included roasters and coffee shop owners and importers, all faith-based to some degree and working in coffee. During a panel conversation, the question was asked about the accountability of how the farmers used the higher prices paid by Christian importers.

I raised my hand from the audience and asked what I supposed was a simple question. "Do you go down and visit them? Do you stay in their house?"

Phoenix Roasters participates in a unique way of doing business we call redemptive trade, a term I coined after researching and discussing the topic with others in the industry.

Redemptive trade is more than business and ministry. It is a relational approach to business that seeks to be friends and family with those whom Phoenix Roasters partners with. When making deals and doing business, both sides need to make money, yes, but the consideration is about more than the individual company's bottom line.

What will this deal mean to the families of those negotiating? What will this deal mean for the workers, the community, the region? For missions? How will our agreement affect employment? Employment and community growth makes for more stable political climates and keeps families from needing to leave and become refugees.

Actions have impacts. That begins with educated consumers purchasing products that do good. Beyond that, businesses and governments must look at the immediate, long-term, and unintended consequences for communities, families, and people.

That is redemptive trade—taking the dignity of exchange and a kingdom mindset that seeks to spread the gospel through missions, preaching, and church planting, while being concerned for the impacts business and politics have on the people God loves. How can business redeem people holistically—spiritually, physically, politically, economically?

As has been said before, Phoenix Roasters never set out to be pioneers or to come up with a cool new term like *redemptive trade*. Phoenix Roasters moved forward with a desperate vision from God to dignify and reach all people, everyone, in every circumstance, that transformation would happen best in deep community where people love, forgive, serve, and find purpose with one another. Together.

God continued to move, giving more than they expected. Phoenix Roasters had the stories. They only needed more places to start sharing them.

Exploration

There are some videos that always get me. Any clip that shows a person getting a pair of special glasses and seeing color for the first time is one that puts a tear in my eye. There is excitement and joy to weeping at seeing everything anew.

Seeing life through the view of the kingdom is like that. We see the same things but now view them through a different lens that gives vibrancy and depth to objects and people and situations. Temporary things are now seen through the perspective of eternity and love.

When the disciples asked Jesus to teach them how to pray like He did, He gave them the model prayer, what some call the Lord's Prayer (Matthew 6:9–13). The prayer begins with a desire for the kingdom above all else, moves into requests, and then ends with another declaration of the kingdom of God.

In writing an essay, the main theme and argument is stated in the introduction and the conclusion. The body of the essay makes points to support that argument. By including the kingdom at the beginning and end of the prayer, Jesus teaches us to ask and pray with the kingdom in view. What would change if we prayed to God seeking the kingdom first? The Alpha and Omega, as it were.

Praying in context of the kingdom sees the request from the perspective of heaven and what God has already accomplished in His authority and power. We *start* from a place of peace, victory, and blessing, not trying to achieve those goals. Kingdom thinking is concerned with the redemption of all things, every person in every situation for eternal good. No request is too small or too great.

Take time to pray over requests, whether small or great, with the kingdom of God as the context and the goal. How has seeking the kingdom first in those requests changed how and what you pray for? Write down one example of how the kingdom mindset adjusted how you prayed.

_____

_____

_____

_____

_____

_____

_____

_____

_____

_____

_____

_____

_____

_____

_____

_____

CHAPTER 13

Coffee That Matters

Tommy and Mimi Holland told Brian a story they heard at a dinner for an organization where they had served as board members.

A businessman had just made the biggest sale of his life in Europe, worth millions of dollars. The kind of sale that set him up for life.

He was excited, feeling like he had achieved the peak of his career.

With his head held a little higher, he boarded the airplane to return from Europe, and he took his seat. Soon an old woman in simple clothes walked on the plane and sat in the one empty seat next to him. He recognized her immediately—Mother Teresa.

What do you say to a living saint? She sat there quietly. Then she turned, laid her hand on his arm, and asked him a simple question.

"Well, son. What do you do that matters?"

This highly successful man who just made gobs of money couldn't answer her. He had no idea. The answer, if he could voice it, was nothing. He couldn't think of one thing.

That moment changed his life. He couldn't do what he did before. He quit his job and set out to initiate a program at Mercer University south of Atlanta. Mercer on Mission takes college students and sends them on mission trips in association with their major.

Tommy shared that story while Brian and Phoenix Roasters prepared for a second pitch meeting with Chick-fil-A in May 2013—this time to become the coffee for the national chain, and Brian developed the catchphrase, *Coffee That Matters*. Phoenix Roasters coffee changed lives in the US through relief at the Atlanta mission and church planting, as well as internationally through missions and direct trade and sustainable wages. It mattered. Buying and drinking the coffee mattered.

Ultimately Phoenix Roasters wasn't chosen to be the coffee for Chick-fil-A. From that process, however, came the catchphrase and hashtag that would be on everything from bags to mugs to T-shirts to social media posts. Phoenix Roasters has since copyrighted #CoffeeThatMatters.

The door to Chick-fil-A might have closed, but others were about to open for Phoenix Roasters to tell their story. Thousands would see *Coffee That Matters* at conferences all over the country.

Why Is She Calling Us?

Angie Ivey from ReThink Group, Inc. and The Orange Conference called Greg Sweatt.

Phoenix had been doing the Conclave and Send conferences, but while they were great opportunities and there had been positive growth, the time and effort involved with serving coffee at conferences caused Greg and Brian to reevaluate the future and participating in these events.

A month after a serious conversation about ceasing to serve at conferences, Greg got the call from Angie. The Orange Conference wanted to change who served coffee at the event, and they had heard about Phoenix Roasters.

ReThink Group, Inc. has their offices in the Atlanta area, and a married couple who worked for them had been interns with Jeff Bagwell at one of his former churches. Those former interns learned of the desire to change coffee companies and spoke to Angie about Phoenix Roasters.

Greg's first thought was, *why are they calling us?* Phoenix was still a small company and not the size of others that could do the job. The Orange Conference is one of the largest conferences in the country for family ministry teams with thousands of church leaders and volunteers present. It would be an amazing opportunity at a target market but a bigger job than Phoenix Roasters had ever done.

As Greg began talking with Angie, she asked what Phoenix Roasters was all about. What could he tell her about the company?

He told her stories, example after example of how God had led and opened doors and directed the company. Stories about a church for the broken and marginalized, a company that started to pay for church planting and missions, the perfect roaster showing up after eighteen months of prayer, missions, direct trade—all of it.

Amazed at the stories of God's leading and working, she told Greg they were talking with other companies, but she would like to have another phone call later in the week with others from The Orange Conference. Greg agreed.

When they spoke again, Angie requested Greg tell the story of Phoenix to everyone on the call.

He did.

He finished the stories, and the people on the call said, "We didn't expect this."

Angie expressed that she wanted Phoenix Roasters to be the choice.

That same week was the meeting between Jeff Foxworthy and Brian, Greg, Jeff, and Phoenix Roasters leadership when Foxworthy told them to "grind it out." Foxworthy also asked about any other prospects in the works.

Greg talked about the possible opportunity with The Orange Conference but how the final decision hadn't been made yet.

Foxworthy said he knew Reggie Joiner, the CEO of ReThink Group, Inc, and would talk to him. Reggie owed him a favor, he went on, since he wrote the foreword to one of Reggie's books.

By the time word got to Angie that Foxworthy had talked with Reggie about a coffee company they would have to deal with, she got anxious. How would she tell Greg that Phoenix Roasters might not get the contract with The Orange Conference now that another company was involved?

She called Greg and started to explain, but Greg revealed that Phoenix Roasters was the company Foxworthy was calling about. What are the chances? One hundred percent!

Phoenix was offered the contract to serve coffee at the massive Orange Conference.

Without knowing yet exactly how they would do it, Greg said yes.

What Do You Want?

Getting further into the world of coffee and conferences, Phoenix Roasters realized that other companies hadn't served well or done what was promised. Some conferences had bad experiences with coffee companies and were wary about the whole set up.

Phoenix Roasters did figure out how to serve thousands of cups of coffee over a few days in different locations for The Orange Conference. Through the church and other networks, Phoenix Roasters brought in volunteers to help serve the coffee. The pastors met other ministers and prayed for them, asked their story, and told their own. Through hard work, love, and serving every individual, Phoenix Roasters did over and above what they promised while serving an amazing cup of coffee.

And people raved about it.

The second year for The Orange Conference passed, and it was another success. The Catalyst leadership conference began looking for another coffee company as well. They had offices near Phoenix Roasters in Duluth and knew many at The Orange Conference, so they called to set up a meeting.

Brian and Greg invited the Catalyst leadership and staff to the warehouse for the meeting. Pastors, coffee staff, and Catalyst staff all sat around together to talk about what Phoenix Roasters could do for Catalyst.

The heart of both companies aligned so well, and after hearing the story of Phoenix Community and Phoenix Roasters, Catalyst knew they were the right choice.

Greg asked them, "What do you want out of this?"

They answered, "A good cup of coffee."

"No," Greg said. "You want a great cup of coffee."

Yes, they did.

Many conferences brought in cheap coffee that didn't taste great. Money and quantity was an issue. But here was a coffee company that would bring in amazing coffee for thousands of people and serve with dignity and love over and above expectations.

Catalyst had two main events in Atlanta (Catalyst East) and in Los Angeles (Catalyst West). However, they also had several One Day events around the country throughout the year. Would Phoenix Roasters be able to do all of those? That would mean travel to several cities. It was a major commitment.

As you can imagine, Phoenix Roasters said yes.

Many of those spots on the One Day tour had especially bad experiences with the previous coffee company that came in and left a mess at their facilities. Phoenix Roasters understood this and set out to be different.

One particular church in Pennsylvania was skeptical of Phoenix Roasters. The One Day event there sold out, and Catalyst asked if Phoenix Roasters could do a second day.

Phoenix Roasters said yes.

Adding the extra day and making everything work, Phoenix Roasters looked like a hero in the eyes of the church that held the event. A one-time skeptical church hugged necks and told Phoenix Roasters they could come back anytime.

Catalyst East in Atlanta begins with an evening session, and travelers come in throughout the afternoon and even stroll in late. A young woman raced in just after the opening session began, and she begged for some coffee.

During the long drive in, her friend wanted to stop and get some quick coffee, but the young woman told her they had to wait to get to the conference. She had been at Catalyst the year before when Phoenix Roasters had served and knew it was great coffee. The young woman entered the opening session with three cups.

Phoenix Roasters also grew more confident and efficient handing out thousands of cups of coffee at a time. Developing a great reputation with The Orange Conference and Catalyst led to catering opportunities with Northpoint Community Church and their satellite campuses all around Atlanta. Phoenix Roasters also serves at Leadercast and Leadercast Women.

Too often in Christian circles, products and services are offered, but the quality is low, counting on people using those products because it is faith-based or Christian and not because it is an excellent product.

Phoenix Roasters wanted to change that story as well. They wanted to start a coffee company that planted churches for the broken and hurting and supported missions, but they also wanted it to be great coffee. They sought out the best quality along the way. The best coffee doing the greatest good.

"No great cause is worth a sorry cup of coffee," is a common saying around the warehouse.

God has led Phoenix Roasters and Phoenix Community one step after another—all the way from sourcing the best coffee, training by a master roaster, direct trade that dignifies farmers and employers, redeeming communities, to serving the best coffee at the greatest conferences.

But God wasn't done yet.

The Next Wave

More than twenty-five years ago, a former B-52 bomber pilot met Brian while they were both volunteering for a multichurch youth missions experience in Shreveport, Louisiana. While working construction for the experience that week, they swapped stories and became friends on the roof and around the project.

The pilot, Rob Hyde, had an engineering degree, and when his nephew Trey Malone, came to him with an idea of a different way to do coffee, they started designing an infusion system together.

Nitro coffee was the new wave, not even a true wave yet, and innovators were just getting into the industry. For the life of coffee, a new way of brewing hadn't been invented beyond brewing the grounds hot or cold. Infusing cold brew with nitrogen created a whole new experience for coffee lovers.

Rob and Trey needed the best coffee to test their creations, and they called Brian and Phoenix Roasters. Brian and Phoenix Roasters got involved, and seeing the potential and the excitement, started working with Rob and Trey (and their other partner) at Cascade Beverages.

With Phoenix Roasters getting involved, Jackson Fendley, one of the pastors at Phoenix Community, began working with the technology, tweaking it from Phoenix Roasters's end.

Jackson had pastored a church in Lawrenceville, Georgia. God had given him the conviction to focus on discipleship, but when he attempted to transition his church to a different model of ministry, they asked him to leave. The church eventually shut down. Jackson heard about a group of pastors in the county doing something different. He came on to help Greg in Buford and then transitioned to Duluth.

Jackson began working with the coffee company like the rest of the pastors, and his engineering skills added to the quality of the box that infused coffee with nitrogen.

The technology developed to the point that the box could infuse any beverage with nitrogen, and both Cascade Beverages and Phoenix Roasters created other non-coffee drinks that could be sold in coffee shops and restaurants.

A large percentage of people think the coffee culture is cool; however, a much smaller percentage actually like coffee. The coffee-infused craft beverages on nitrogen created a way for others to have an amazing specialty drink while enjoying the cool coffee culture. This was a way to attract people who enjoy the coffee culture but haven't yet found a coffee drink they like.

The nitro coffee and craft beverages come in kegs and are served from a tap like a beer. Nitrogen brings out other flavors and gives the beverage a smoother texture. Along with black coffee, Brian and Phoenix Roasters designed flavored coffees like the Caranilla. Some customers count the coffee-infused nitro craft beverages as their favorites—Blonde Blueberry Basil, the Vanilla Chai, the Raspberry Lemonade, and others are available for shops and restaurants to purchase.

The technology evolved into something significantly unique and superior to other nitro systems. Even beer companies and breweries marveled at the nitro head that stayed on the beverage far longer than any others in the market. Cascade Beverages and Phoenix Roasters began working on a patent with the US government. Along with the patent came other opportunities to partner with larger companies.

Phoenix Roasters has come to expect God to do great things when they say yes to him.

The coffee business wasn't the only thing growing and expanding during that time. Phoenix Community also planted more churches.

Exploration

A healthy person evaluates priorities. There are endless things we can do. What is most important? Some of those priorities will be different to certain individuals depending on the situation or role in life—family, marriage, children, education, etc.

From God's perspective, there are two things we deal with that matter most because they have eternal value. Greg teaches that those two things are the Word of God and the souls of people.

That doesn't mean that other things don't matter—family, work, etc. But with a kingdom perspective in every circumstance, our priorities are the Word of God, his truth, and the souls of people. Those things are eternal.

We see these two over and over in Scripture together, even in the famous John 3:16—"For God so loved the world that he gave his one and only Son, that whoever believes in him shall not perish but have eternal life" (NIV). God loved people so much He sent His Son (the Word, the Truth) so that people wouldn't die but instead have life.

Nothing is more precious to God than His Word and people. Do we value those things in every situation? Our contexts may be different, but the call to the Word and people is universal for those who follow Christ.

Does that change how we treat and value people? What we say to them? How we serve them?

As we say at Phoenix Community—relationships are everything; the rest is just details.

Pray for God to help you value His Word and the relationships in your life more. Write down one way you can actively value each of those two.

_____

_____

_____

_____

_____

_____

_____

_____

_____

_____

_____

_____

_____

_____

_____

_____

CHAPTER 14

Realizing the Vision

Even as a pastor in Duluth, Jeff Bagwell continued to live in Gainesville—forty-five minutes or more away—and built relationships. He wanted to plant a church there at some point, but he and Kelly had to wait until their twins were at a more manageable place.

When Kelly went back to work to help support the family, Jeff took more of the daily responsibilities of raising the twins. He took the boys to school, doctor visits to better diagnose their needs, and occupational therapy appointments. Finding ways to deal with two autistic boys took priority over the years. Jeff did want to plant a church, but his family had to be in the right place first.

Finding more solutions over time, the boys matured and went into high school. The family situation improved with better education and therapy options. Jeff started a small group in his home to develop a core.

Chris Dawkins, one of the longtime leaders and members of Phoenix Community in Duluth, and his wife Lee moved up to Gainesville to be closer to family. They knew as well as anyone what Phoenix Community was about, and they served much as a pastor would over the year that Jeff and Kelly had the community group. Chris is also a great worship leader, an advantage for the new church.

One of the people Jeff had contact with over the years was Benny, the owner of Little Italy Pizza in Gainesville. Benny employed young people at his restaurant, some who needed help and a second chance, much like Phil back at Pepperoni's. He welcomed the new church to meet on the enclosed patio.

The small core of the new church worked to put up equipment they would need to meet out on the patio. And Phoenix Community of Gainesville began meeting in the fall of 2015.

Dance Studio and a Handlebar Mustache

The time at Little Italy was great for Phoenix Community in Gainesville, but they began to grow and needed more space. The model of Phoenix Community is to have at least two pastors at every church; Gainesville also needed a copastor for Jeff.

Luke Pinder arrived as the answer to the second need. Luke had experience with large churches as a youth pastor, and he and Jeff had developed a relationship over the years, even getting to know Phoenix Roasters when Luke worked at a church in Sugar Hill, Georgia.

An outgoing man with a famous handlebar mustache, Luke took a job in Colorado where he worked as the youth pastor. He enjoyed the time in Colorado but experienced much of the same frustrations with the "bigger, better" push from the head pastor and leadership.

In the spring of 2017, Luke and the church in Colorado parted ways. Discouraged and wondering what would be next, Jeff offered the idea that Luke could come and be copastor in Gainesville. Luke and his wife Joy prayed and thought about it.

They said yes and moved their young family from Colorado to Gainesville, Georgia, and joined the team.

A coffee shop in Gainesville used Phoenix Roasters coffee and sold the nitro craft beverages. A popular spot for people downtown in the morning through lunch, Midland Station was owned by a local church. Midland had a stage and sound system for live music, so Phoenix Community in Gainesville met there for six months.

The local church was kind to let Phoenix Community in Gainesville meet there, but it was always going to be a temporary situation. The larger church wanted to plant their own church at some point. Jeff and Luke had become friends with Justin, who owned a dance studio two doors down from Midland Station. Justin enjoyed the coffee and story of Phoenix Community and told Jeff that the church could meet at the dance studio.

Phoenix Community in Gainesville moved two doors down and started meeting there. Eventually Justin let the church build out an unfinished space at the studio for them to use every Sunday.

The Gainesville Community

Tony and Heather Jonovitch work in food service, so they usually had events on Sundays. They came to the church when they could but asked Jeff if he would lead a Bible study at their business. Opening the study up to the employees, Jeff teaches on Tuesdays at 2:30 p.m.

A primary avenue of service for Phoenix Community in Gainesville is their involvement with the ministry Good News at Noon, an outreach and shelter for the homeless in the city. Jeff, Luke, and the church show up to serve a meal and lead worship on the third Saturday of the month. Other churches are involved too, and they serve during the month.

With Good News at Noon located close enough to walk, people can come to church at the dance studio. Some come and never return. A few stay, and Phoenix Community begins relationships with them to start seeing transformation.

Phoenix Community in Gainesville has helped one man get a job and housing. Relationship is the key to transformation, and he's eaten Thanksgiving dinner with the Bagwells and was baptized at the church.

Now Phoenix Community in Gainesville has three community groups and continues to build relationships with people in the downtown area and around Gainesville.

Kelly Bagwell has transitioned from her job at the public school and is now a licensed counselor. Some of her clients are pastors from bigger churches experiencing the burnout and struggles she and Jeff knew years ago.

A Different Path

My wife Becca and I took a bit of a different path to Phoenix Community. When we met and got married, we spoke often about working overseas.

Becca is fluent in German and worked as a German teacher, and I also worked in the public school system, so we always assumed we would move to Europe to teach internationally.

But when a friend set up a meeting with a missions organization about moving to East Asia, we both felt a call from God to go.

It took research and time to find the right school. We were offered a job in Seoul, a great opportunity in a major city, but when we prayed about it, God told us that wasn't the place for us.

Discouraged, I signed my contract for the next school year thinking all the options were done. Becca didn't sign hers with the faith God had told us we would be somewhere else the next year. Close to the end of the school year, another opportunity in Korea opened up, and we were offered a job in the smaller city of Pyeongtaek.

We said yes, and in 2002 we moved to Korea.

Missions taught us about the transformative power of community and relationships. In our third year, we took over a ministry to the military called the Hospitality House. The Hospitality House serves meals on Friday and Saturday nights and holds worship and Bible studies through the week in conjunction with the chapel on nearby Osan Air Base.

Even though many of the military and expats were only there for a year or two, we saw amazing transformation in young men and women and families. People from all denominations set aside minor theological differences and spent time together, loving one another and living life with each other.

The common element in those who changed drastically? Community. Living life with others of the faith.

I also started getting more intentional about discipleship in Korea, mentoring future leaders and discipling young men and seeing them grow in their gifts.

When we returned from Korea in 2006, Becca and I came to the US with a passion to live like missionaries in the country of our birth, to take the principles of community and discipleship and teach others how to live on mission for God in America.

We didn't get involved with large churches. God had always led us to smaller, more intimate and community-oriented gatherings. Back in America, that was no different. We started a house church and networked with other house churches and ministries in Atlanta.

Those years with the house church movement were both difficult and amazing times. We saw God work in so many ways, but the season came to an end as a few families within our house church moved to other cities or felt led to go to a different church. In a larger church, seeing a few families leave can be sad, but it's not debilitating to the ministry. With a house church, that same number is more than three-fourths of the group.

I wanted to expand the house church network, raise up more leaders, and see the simple community-oriented model grow. I then felt God change the season, and the vision seemed to die when the house church ended.

At the same time, I lost my day job, which supported my family while I did ministry with the house church. Unemployed during the hard economy of the recession, I struggled to find another job. I got back into public school after receiving my masters, but I knew public education wasn't what God had for me.

Discouraged at seeing a dream die out, Becca and I visited pastor friends in the city but knew we needed a place to call home.

Phoenix Suwanee

My mother and sisters had been at the same church with Brian Holland years ago, and I, along with my sister and brother-in-law, had led worship at youth events and later for the first year at Phoenix Community of Atlanta at Pepperoni's. We became close family friends.

Phoenix Community possessed many of the same ideas Becca and I loved about house church—bivocational ministry, simple organization, focus on community. With the experience we had as missionaries overseas, were were influenced by *When Helping Hurts* and similar ideas for missions and mission trips. We also loved the added dimension of reaching out to the broken and hurting and the poor.

We prayed, and God told us to start attending Phoenix Community of Atlanta in Duluth. Like Greg Sweatt before us, Becca and I didn't want to be leaders or pastors. We needed time to heal and get involved with the families and people in Duluth.

Time passed, and we started a community group. Later Brian and the church invited me to work for the coffee company and come on staff. Then I became more intentional about discipleship, even writing my own material to address identifying spiritual gifts and the importance of living on mission with God from the new creation identity.

Planting a church was always part of the discussion, and as the church in Duluth grew to standing-room only again and the young people I had discipled were discipling others, an opportunity at a business with a small meeting room opened up in Suwanee, where Becca and I lived. Wes and Sarah Wood, a young couple who had been involved with Phoenix since the beginning, were excited about being copastors with us, and they also lived in Suwanee.

Would we plant a Phoenix church in Suwanee?

We said yes.

A Church in a Brewery

After a short stint meeting in a small private school, I became friends with Veugeler Design Group, the company responsible for the website for Phoenix Roasters. Veugeler started talking about a new dream they had—opening a craft brewery right in downtown Suwanee, taking over the old fire station. It was an amazing location.

I asked them what time they would open on Sundays. Probably not until 12:30pm or so, they answered.

What would they think of a church meeting in the brewery on Sunday mornings?

It was not something they had been thinking about, but the conversations continued. The new brewery, StillFire, put in some taps with Phoenix Roaster's nitro craft beverages and had a vision to be a community space that was dog and kid friendly, and they agreed to let Phoenix Suwanee meet on Sunday mornings.

Phoenix Suwanee started meeting at the brewery in the fall of 2019.

We at the church focus on making disciples who make disciples. I have continued to develop my materials and have taken several from the fellowship through it, meeting in small groups and finding deeper community as they connect on the redemptive purpose of God. A few have committed to taking what they have learned and starting their own groups.

Wes Wood now works at the Potter's House in Jefferson, Georgia, a sister ministry to the Atlanta Mission downtown. Phoenix Community in Suwanee has done several events at the Potter's House, focused on beginning and maintaining relationships with the men overcoming addiction and homelessness there.

For the last two years, the church has cooked and served Thanksgiving dinner to the men in the Potter's House program who aren't at the point where they can leave the facility. Their families can come to spend time with them, so the church provides the dinner for those families to have time together and a nice Thanksgiving with one another.

But like all the Phoenix Community fellowships, we have made friends with neighbors who have come to the church. Becca works at the high school in Suwanee, and with those connections, we build relationships and reach out to the hurting to bring relief.

It all starts with making friends.

Making Friends and Intentionally Teaching Them about Jesus

The mission of the Phoenix Community of Atlanta is to "Make friends and intentionally teach them about Jesus." This simple statement allows for diversity and individuality but drives the heart behind all that is done at Phoenix Community churches.

Phoenix Community in Duluth is involved in working with the community through a Tuesday night meal and community group for the whole church. People come to have deeper discussions about the message on Sunday or the series. It is a good time to invite friends to the church.

For years Brian and his son Duke volunteered every other Saturday for WellSpring Living, an organization that helps women at risk or victimized by sexual exploitation. Brian and Duke moved heavy furniture that had been donated to the ministry. Even during difficult times for Duke, that was a good space for them to connect as father and son.

The warehouse in Duluth, where the Phoenix Community in Duluth meets on Sunday, is used during the week for other events or ministries that have included "holy" yoga, a youth meeting, and a sewing class, a time where older and younger women connect and encourage each other while making crafts together.

Once Jeff and I left Duluth to plant churches, Jackson Fendley came to Duluth as the copastor there. Brian and Jackson spend Tuesday mornings at the Atlanta Mission leading men through Bible studies. They've even gone through T4T, Training for Trainers, a discipleship material that Jackson has found important.

Every Christmas, Brian and the Phoenix Community in Atlanta organize a massive breakfast for the men at the Atlanta Mission. Those who volunteer arrive at the Mission at 4:30 a.m. on Christmas morning to prepare scrambled eggs, sausages, blueberry pancakes, juice, and amazing coffee. Both the men from the shelter and those in the program come and sit down and are served by the volunteers. People are encouraged to sit down and take the time to get names and stories from the men, to dignify them with relationship.

Whether reaching out to neighbors, coworkers, or avenues of relief, the goal remains the same—to make friends and intentionally teach them about Jesus.

Exploration

I love to travel. From my time overseas to now, I have had amazing experiences in different countries on mission trips and simply seeing the world. My wife and I even bring our kids on these trips to different states or events. We call them adventures.

Followers of Jesus are sent-people.

What we call the Great Commission is when Jesus sent the disciples out to declare the good news of the kingdom. In Matthew 28, Jesus told them to go and make disciples. The commission in the Gospel of John 20:21 is simpler—"As the Father has sent me, so I am sending you."

For Phoenix Community, engagement in the community around us and missions is crucial. It is the heart of the idea of "marketplace church." Our goal to make friends and intentionally teach them about Jesus requires us to go.

This isn't the call for pastors only. It is for all Christ followers.

You don't have to go overseas or lead a big meeting. God may be sending you to coworkers or neighbors. But if you are a follower of Christ, you are being sent somewhere.

Pray to the Father, and ask Him where He has sent you. Write down a list of relationships, places, or situations that God has sent you to be a light.

_____

_____

_____

_____

_____

_____

_____

_____

_____

_____

_____

_____

CHAPTER 15

Bigger than You Think

It began with a random call at 4 p.m. on a Friday.
Tired and ready for the weekend, Brian didn't want to take the call, but he did. A woman on the other end began to explain that she was from an Ethiopian coffee company, UUMA, looking for roasting partners.

Phoenix Roasters had been seeking an Ethiopian coffee partner, or a partner from another African country. But Brian knew what Phoenix Roasters needed would be a hard sell, and, frankly, he was exhausted. He ran through the list of what Phoenix Roasters looks for in a coffee partner, principles God had taught them over the years—high-quality specialty coffee and farmers who want to help the community or others in a missional way.

Brian expected a polite but quick goodbye from the woman.

Instead she said, "You must talk to my husband."

Her husband got on the phone, and Brian repeated what Phoenix Roasters looks for in a coffee farm. And that they only work with these farmers directly.

The man from UUMA heard the pitch, a unique set of standards, and he told Brian, "I can't wait for you to meet my father."

Brian began to arrange a trip to Ethiopia to meet this family and see the farm.

When he arrived he learned UUMA has plans to build a school and church closer to their coffee farm. Currently the approximately twenty thousand people in the local community have to travel two hours to school or church and two hours back.

UUMA had also recently added a bean-washing station for their company and made it available to other smaller farmers in the area, which helps the economics of the whole community.

The farm and family of Ethiopia aligned with the Phoenix Roasters vision.

The Birthplace of Coffee

Brian went on a trip to the farm in Ethiopia. He took his father, a member from the Phoenix Community in Duluth, and an old friend. After staying in a hotel in the capital city of Addis Ababa, they traveled down to the UUMA farm close to the Sudan border. The plan was to only be there for a day.

Plans often change, however.

Muddy roads made the journey difficult, and Brian's father Tommy couldn't make it the last half mile to visit the farm since the rest of the group had to hike through mud and rain to get there. Brian and the rest of the group enjoyed the visit with the coffee farm family, but they were eager to get back to their hotel and out of the muddy clothes. They reunited with Tommy and made it back to the southern Ethiopian town of Mizan.

At dinner that night they were told of a protest between their location and their flight out, and the group was going to have to stay another night in Mizan. The small town was swelling with people who weren't planning on staying another night. While Brian and the Americans were in the southern part of the country, other Ethiopian leaders and dignitaries met to discuss important economic issues with the coffee industry, like transportation and trade. Now everyone was in the same situation. Stuck.

One day turned into two. Two into three. And on the third day the group decided to try and make it out. At four in the morning a caravan of fifty vehicles full of dignitaries and businessmen and Brian, Tommy, and their group were escorted by seven military trucks outfitted with .50 caliber guns on top. Each of the vehicles had five to eight soldiers outfitted with automatic weapons.

Not long into the journey, protesters started blocking the road with trees and burning barricades.

Keffa is a region in Ethiopia that has long been considered the birthplace and origin of coffee. That region was split into two states by the government, and now both states claim they are the birthplace for coffee. The protesters decided to disrupt travel by these dignitaries to claim the title of origin of coffee. Brian, Tommy, and the others just happened to be in the wrong place and time and stuck in the middle of the conflict.

The group from Phoenix Roasters had left their bags in the hotel in Addis Ababa, thinking they'd be back within a day. Now they had been stuck in the same clothes for days.

Even with the military assistance, they couldn't make it far on the road and had to stay in a hotel in a smaller town. The protest delayed their trip back by four days, and Brian and the group were in danger of missing their flight home. Finally, with help from the United Nations, the group was brought back to the city by a small private plane to Addis Ababa, where they were able to catch their flight back to the United States.

Everyone made it out of the country safely and on time.

With an office for UUMA in Atlanta and a new relationship with excellent natural specialty coffee, the relationship with Ethiopia has only begun. Brian and Phoenix Roasters look forward to more relief and generosity through the partnership.

Not What You Expect

Phoenix Roasters and Cascade Beverages joined together in a business venture called Cuatro Connect to get the patent for the unique process to infuse beverages with nitrogen. The patent brought Phoenix Roasters into conversations with larger companies that saw the potential in the best technology for nitro infusion and the security of a legal protection from competitors.

The first company Phoenix Roasters signed an agreement with was Curtis, a large coffee equipment manufacturer. Once the nitro technology was out there, Phoenix Roasters ran into a new problem—protecting the investment and the patent for the technology.

Another major company with connections in the nitro coffee industry, MicroMatic, wanted access to the technology. A conflict began with talk of lawyers and letters and legal action.

What was one of the principles that Phoenix operated by? Relationships are everything. The rest is just details.

Before taking major legal action, Brian and Phoenix Roasters asked this second company in for a meeting to begin a relationship.

The president of the company later said he had never heard of another company wanting to meet and negotiate face-to-face and not through lawyers. Executives from MicroMatic flew into Atlanta and came to the Phoenix Roasters warehouse. The owners of Phoenix Roasters and Rob from Cascade Beverages began telling their story, the story of Phoenix Roasters and Cascade, their heart and purpose. Phoenix and Cascade ended with a proposition—what if we could be friends and partners in this industry instead of enemies?

The president of MicroMatic looked at the group and said, "I wasn't expecting this."

The conversation continued, however, to the point that several executives from MicroMatic went on a trip to Guatemala with Brian to see the impact of redemptive trade on the communities there.

Relationships matter.

Why Am I Here?

While growth and transition are positive, they also create opportunities for conflict and stress.

The Phoenix Roasters ownership met with their new accountant in 2017, and she had some hard truths for Phoenix Roasters. They were growing and making money, but if they didn't tighten their expenditures, they would be closed in six months. The accountant told them they needed to transition from a small, mom-and-pop company to a more structured and organized operation. The current path wasn't sustainable.

It was a shock to the whole group, but Brian especially took it personally. He and Greg had a sharp disagreement, and hurtful things were said.

That same year, Phoenix Community in Buford decided to restructure into a home discipleship group. Attendance had been lacking, and despite the hard work of Greg and Wes and the other leaders, they collectively decided to end the church plant until they could strategize a new way to reach out in the community.

They all agreed, but this felt like a failure instead of strategic reorganization. And it hurt. After the difficult meeting with the new accountant and the hard conversation with Brian, Greg prayed for two weeks about whether or not he should quit.

Greg believes relationships are everything, and he would rather get out of the business so he and Brian could remain friends. The coffee business was a passion, but it wasn't more important than friendship. He and Julie decided to sign everything they had in Phoenix Roasters over to the business and quit.

Early one Saturday morning, he prayed and spent time with God. During that time, God brought Everett Miller to Greg's mind.

Everett had been involved with Phoenix Roasters from the beginning. Greg and Everett shared a hotel in Guatemala on one of the first trips, and while staying together, Everett asked what he could pray for Greg about.

Greg answered, "Pray my pride never gets in the way between me and Brian."

He did pray for Greg that night.

Now, years later, Greg thought of his friend. He couldn't call him like he usually did when God put people on his mind. Everett served in missions overseas. So Greg prayed for Everett.

Then Everett called him.

"What are you doing?" Everett asked on the phone.

"Praying for you," Greg said.

"What's your address?" Everett said.

"Why?"

Everett was in fact not overseas but was sitting in his car at an exit a couple miles from Greg's house in Buford.

Greg texted the address, and then went to the next room to get Julie.

His wife had heard the stories over the years—from ministry and mission trips and the coffee business—and she had been jealous of those God moments.

Julie was up praying too. He told her she should get ready. A God moment was about to happen.

Greg made coffee, and he, Julie, and Everett sat together that Saturday morning.

"Tell me why I'm here," Everett said.

"I don't know," Greg said. "I prayed for you."

"Tell me what's been going on," Everett said.

"Remember when I asked you to pray for me and my pride with Brian?"

He did.

Greg explained the situation and the difficult owners' meeting with the accountant.

Everett knew why he was there.

"Why?" Greg asked.

Everett told him a story of four men he knew when he was in a church in Mobile, Alabama, years before and had worked with at AT&T in the cellular industry. They were great friends, and they lived life together.

AT&T shut down their division and gave the men severance. The men didn't have work but did have some time to figure out their next steps with the severance. One of the men was up early praying and God gave him the direction. He took this idea to his friends.

The money in the cellular industry wasn't in cell phones but in the cell towers. They could go out to the places they knew and had been researching as potential cell tower properties, buy the properties, and put towers on them.

That's what they did.

Later on, one of the men wanted out. The first man, the one with the idea, begged him not to sell, encouraged him that the big payday was coming. The second man sold anyway.

One by one, each came and sold their ownership to the first man.

He begged each of them to stay, but in the end, the first man alone owned the company.

The payday did come in the form of several million dollars. The other three men resented the first man with the idea. None of the four men talk to each other anymore.

Everett told Greg, "I'm here to tell you, 'Don't quit.' It's bigger than you think."

Greg didn't quit.

Soon after that conversation with Everett, the nitro patent came through, opening up major doors with bigger companies. Along with the patent, other opportunities for coffee shops and distribution increased.

In early 2018, God woke Greg up with a list of things to get done to get the business in better shape, to work more efficiently, and be better structured for success.

Phoenix Roasters didn't close in six months.

It was bigger than he thought.

Exploration

When we say yes to God, we walk a path of purpose and intimacy. We encounter struggles and miracles and creative new ideas. On the path, we realize His purpose was bigger than we thought.

Paul speaks of this in 1 Corinthians 2:9, "No eye has seen, no ear has heard, and no mind has imagined what God has prepared for those who love him."

It's bigger than we think.

Growing up, the teaching usually stopped with that verse. We can't know what God is doing, right?

If we continue to verse 10, however, Paul says, "But it was to us that God revealed these things by his Spirit."

As we walk with God, He reveals His plans through His Spirit. It may take time or a God moment with a friend, but He reveals His plans to those who follow Him. And they are big plans. Redemptive plans. Good plans. Bigger than we thought.

Think of a current situation you feel called to that may be difficult.

Pray for strength to be faithful and seek His revelation for what His purpose is within that struggle. Write down what God shared with you about His purpose within the difficult time.

_____

_____

_____

_____

_____

_____

_____

_____

_____

_____

_____

_____

_____

_____

_____

_____

_____

_____

_____

CHAPTER 16
Not the End

Ministry and coffee are a great combo. The Phoenix Community pastors have the dream job, right? While working at conferences like Catalyst and The Orange Conference, people come up to Brian and the Phoenix Community pastors often and express their jealousy.

Working in coffee is far from a glamorous life, which includes getting up at 3 a.m. to brew coffee for those starting their day early at 7 a.m. for an event or school or conference. Organizations and churches have events while others have time off in the evenings and weekends, events where they want coffee or hot chocolate or even decaf.

Roasting is a hot, laborious process. Lifting and moving heavy bags of bean, measuring out bean into buckets, repeating the same process over and over for hours on end.

The production staff works long shifts grinding bean, filling bags of all sizes and types, putting together orders, and shipping them.

That doesn't begin to account for the time spent in ministry counseling, pastoring, discipling, and having community with church families.

Phoenix Community believes in what God has done and continues to do through the coffee and church planting and missions. They witness transformation on a regular basis, stories that inspire them and others of God moving in the lives of people.

At times it is difficult work, however. The secret is to keep showing up and keep being faithful with what God has given them to do, whether relationships or coffee or ministry. Saying yes isn't a one-time event. Disciples and followers of Christ say yes every day and keep saying yes in obedience to what God has directed them to do.

And because Christ followers believe God is responsible for the consequences, they know the story isn't over quite yet.

The story is still being written.

The foundation of the story remains the same. Say yes to God. Trust Him with the consequences and the results. Be faithful in obedience, weather the storms of life, and watch as God increases favor and influence for His glory and the good of His children.

It is bigger than anyone originally thought. In a time when the coffee company was young and there was no roaster or source of green bean, Brian, Greg, and Jeff couldn't have imagined serving at The Orange Conference with thousands in attendance, much less traveling around the country with Catalyst.

Now Phoenix Roasters counts those organizations as family, continually striving to bring value to those leadership events. The catering business has boomed with schools and churches like Northpoint in the Atlanta area. Phoenix Roasters serves excellent coffee and tells God's story all around the city.

In 2019 Phoenix Roasters served coffee to thousands of volunteers at the Passion Conference at the Mercedes-Benz Stadium in Atlanta, the beginning of another relationship.

ReThink has begun a new project building Phase Family Centers, facilities that support church planting, shared work spaces, meeting rooms, and a private school. They invited Phoenix Roasters to run the coffee shop at the first Phase Family Center, which opened in August 2019.

Other plans for coffee shops and partnerships with retail spaces are on the horizon.

Brian's daughter Emily Ryan now works in marketing and branding with Phoenix Roasters. She graduated from Mercer University and gets to bring value to the company her father started.

Years ago, leaders and pastors of Phoenix Community sat around and talked about a marketplace church. That dream was for a coffee shop or a single space to engage the community. Now Phoenix Roasters is served in churches, coffee shops, and restaurants around the country.

With nitro craft beverages and the unique patented infusion technology, Phoenix Roasters has been thrust even further into the marketplace. Nitro has opened doors the roasted coffee never had with equipment manufacturers, other coffee shops, bars, and breweries. Connecting with other businesses, selling delicious flavors and high-quality technology, allows for more relationships and opportunities to show grace and integrity outside of the typical church world.

Five dollars from every keg Phoenix Roasters sells goes to help the homeless at the Atlanta Mission. Phoenix brings in partners, working together to bring relief and hope through business.

All of these are opportunities to tell the story. To tell God's story. To bring transformation in the lives of people and plant more churches.

Greg Sweatt has started a small group in his home in his community in Buford. He hasn't given up reaching out to his neighbors and showing love to those around him.

Phoenix Community in Athens began in 2020 and ministers to students at the University of Georgia, discipling and creating community there.

Phoenix Roasters continues to see communities transform in Panama, Guatemala, Honduras, and Ethiopia. The Caballeros in Panama add more pastors and missionaries to their support list. San Juan Moca improves with better education and a higher standard of hygiene and health. Phoenix Roasters is brainstorming creative ways to add more dignity through vocation and supports church planting and other ministry efforts in other places in Guatemala as well. In Honduras, the co-op succeeds in getting more families to a self-sustaining life and plants more churches in the beautiful mountains. UUMA in Ethiopa grows and collects resources to build a church and a school.

And there's still more to do. Phoenix hasn't figured it all out yet. In coffee, business, missions, and church planting, God is faithful to give direction and help to those who stay humble and willing to grow and get better.

Listen to the Father. He gives direction and insight, making connections with individuals and organizations to work together for the kingdom.

The plan for moving forward is simple. It's the same as the plan that brought Phoenix Community and Phoenix Roasters this far. They will hear God speak. And they will say yes.

Exploration

The story isn't over.

Your story isn't over.

I remember having a pity party after losing my job and seeing a ministry fade and close. I felt like a failure, and I was ready to quit. This was all over, right?

My two-year-old daughter came to me with a children's book on the story of Joseph. She opened to the page where his brothers threw him into a pit. "That must have made him feel bad," she said.

"Yeah," I answered.

Then she turned to the back of the book where Joseph is the second in command of Egypt and embracing his brothers in reconciliation and restoration. "But look," my daughter said. "It all turned out okay in the end."

Okay, I told God. *I get it. I won't quit.*

It is normal to feel that the story is over, especially when tragedy strikes. We feel stuck, or it doesn't seem like there's any way out.

In the Book of Ruth, Naomi lost her husband and sons, and when she returned to Israel, she changed her name to Mara, which means "bitterness," for "the Almighty has made life very bitter for me" (Ruth 1:20–21). She thought her tragedy was the end of her family.

But Ruth, her widowed daughter-in-law, wouldn't leave her. After interacting with Boaz in the community, he married and redeemed Ruth. Naomi saw God work wonderful things for her, giving her a grandson and joy in her old age.

If you're in that place of desperation and discouragement, we at Phoenix Community have been there. There are days and times we still struggle and wonder what's going to happen next. How will God show up this time?

Keep saying yes. There's more to do.

Revisit your story, the dreams from God you've written down, and ways that He has helped you overcome in the past. Pray with the Spirit for more faith and grace. You're invited to freely come before the throne of grace to get more grace (Hebrews 4:16). Go boldly.

As you look over the things you've written while reading this book, collect the words from God and the dreams He has given you. Put them in a place where you will revisit them and pray over them and pray from them.

We are praying with you.

_____

_____

_____

_____

_____

_____

_____

_____

_____

_____

_____

_____

_____

CONCLUSION

Jesus is the yes.

There is power in saying yes to God because we are participating in the work of the Spirit of Jesus.

In Revelation 3:14, Jesus identifies Himself to the church at Laodicea as "the one who is the Amen—the faithful and true witness, the beginning of God's new creation." The Apostle Paul declares that in Christ, all God's promises are yes (2 Corinthians 1:20). In the Gospels, Jesus testified that He did nothing of Himself, that He did what He saw the Father doing (John 5:19).

Jesus lived every moment in yes to God, and He is the great teacher, the one who provided the way back into relationship with the Father. Upon our repentance and commitment, the Spirit of Christ is given to us, and we are reborn in that power. Empowered with the yes to the Father.

This is not a story about coffee or business or even church and missions. It is not one person's story.

It is God's story, the one He is telling.

He tells His story through the lives of people, those transformed by His love, the broken and hurting and addicted and marginalized finding purpose and life in the love of the Father. The people that rise from the ashes of life to be a light in this world, a beacon of hope for others.

The secret of the Phoenix Community and Phoenix Roasters story is not in a method for church planting or missions or redemptive trade in business. Those principles have come from God and speak of the kingdom, but those secrets alone have the temptation to become another script to blindly follow apart from relationship. Another word for that is *religion* or *legalism*, even in the name of good.

Phoenix Community didn't get this far by following someone else's script.

The secret is hearing from God, saying yes to Him, and trusting Him with the consequences. Trusting that He is good, that He is about the kingdom for all people.

What can you expect if you'll say yes to Him?

Your life will be a unique and creative expression of Jesus to the world, a supernatural declaration through God's working in and through lives. It will be bigger than you think. Your story will bring hope to others and inspire them to do the same.

Say yes to God. It won't be easy. But it will be worth it.

ACKNOWLEDGMENTS

The Phoenix Community and Phoenix Roasters story would not have been possible without hundreds and thousands of people saying yes. These are but a few whose stories have intersected and propelled what God is doing through Phoenix Community and Phoenix Roasters.

To the Phoenix Community pastors and their wives: Brian and Ginney Holland, Jeff and Kelly Bagwell, Greg and Julie Sweatt, Wes and Becky Patterson, Britt and Becca Mooney, Jackson and Chris Fendley, Luke and Joy Pinder, and Wes and Sarah Wood.

To the children and families of the pastors who also made sacrifices for the vision of the church and the company.

To Tommy and Mimi Holland and Jim "Pop" and Sarah Dukes.

To Rob and Lisa Brooks, Barry Owen, Charles Stanley, Lester "Duke" Harris, Phil Brown, Chris and Lee Dawkins, Morgan Lopes, Ben and Gina Deaton, Jason and Shane Ardell, Ken and Pam Morrow, and Kevin and Sonya Morgan.

To Joe Wingo, Benny Cotese, Justin and Danielle Holland, and Andreas van Honk.

To Mark Adams, Hunter Lambeth, Steve and Ruth Nolen, Perry Walker, Robert Lupton, Everett Miller, John Malone, Randall and Angela Vuegeler, Walt Wooden, Jerrill Sprinkle, and Eugene Brisco.

To Mario Mejia, Elias and Lorenzo Caballero, Irving Navichoc, Pastor Rafael Puac Trejo and Maria, Greg, and Jean Hines, Javier Pitti, and UUMA.

To Angie Ivey, Daniel Cline, Leadercast, The Atlanta Mission, and The Potter's House.

To Ken and Beth Roe.

To Rob Hyde, Trey Malone, and Cian Hickey.

To Jeff Foxworthy.

For this book and the author, these people made it possible: my agent Cyle Young, my publisher John Herring and the wonderful team at Iron Stream Media (Ramona Richards, Reagan Jackson, and Tina Atchenson), and Bethany Jett and Michelle Medlock Adams for teaching me about how generosity is its own success.

To Becca, my love and my partner in this life, and to Micah, Elisha, and Hosanna, thank you for your patience and willingness to work together in this crazy kingdom adventure.

To the Great Storyteller, the God who redeems and raises us all from the ashes to new life, this belongs to you.

ABOUT THE AUTHOR

In the second grade, Britt Mooney sat with nothing to do on Friday while others in his class had to retake a test, and he kept getting in trouble. His teacher said, "Britt, why don't you write me a story?" He thought that was the greatest idea he ever heard and proceeded to write her a story every Friday. He hasn't stopped writing since.

Britt grew up in Georgia, taught overseas in the Republic of Korea, traveled the world on mission, and returned to eventually work for a coffee company and plant a church in a brewery. He lives in Suwanee, Georgia, with his amazing wife Becca, their three kids, and a dog. He writes both fiction and nonfiction.

Check out his website: www.mbmooney.com

Follow on social media: www.facebook.com/mooneymb and www.instagram.com/authormbmooney

For great discussions on the kingdom of God and how God transforms lives, listen to the Kingdom Over Coffee Podcast: www.facebook.com/kingdomovercoffee

Connect with Phoenix Roasters

Phoenix Roasters website: www.phoenixroasters.coffee

Facebook: www.facebook.com/phoenixroasterscoffee

Instagram: www.instagram.com/phoenixroasters

Phoenix Community of Atlanta website: www.phoenixatl.org

**If you enjoyed this book,
will you consider sharing the message with others?**

Let us know your thoughts at info@ironstreammedia.com.
You can also let the author know by visiting or sharing a photo
of the cover on our social media pages or leaving a review at a
retailer's site. All of it helps us get the message out!

Facebook.com/IronStreamMedia

———————

Iron Stream Books, New Hope® Publishers, Ascender Books, and
New Hope Kidz are imprints of Iron Stream Media,
which derives its name from Proverbs 27:17,
"As iron sharpens iron, so one person sharpens another."

This sharpening describes the process of discipleship, one to
another. With this in mind, Iron Stream Media provides a variety
of solutions for churches, ministry leaders, and nonprofits ranging
from in-depth Bible study curriculum and Christian book
publishing to custom publishing and consultative services. Through
our popular Life Bible Study, Student Life Bible Study brands, and
New Hope imprints, ISM provides web-based full-year and short-
term Bible study teaching plans as well as printed devotionals,
Bibles, and discipleship curriculum.

For more information on ISM and Iron Stream Books,
please visit
IronStreamMedia.com